QBASIC™
FOR ROOKIES

Clayton Walnum

QBasic for Rookies

Copyright © 1993 by Que® Corporation

Library of Congress Catalog No.: 93-84126

ISBN: 1-56529-235-9

95 94 93   6 5 4 3 2 1

Interpretation of the printing code: the rightmost double-digit number is the year of the book's printing; the rightmost single-digit number, the number of the book's printing. For example, a printing code of 93-1 shows that the first printing of the book occurred in 1993.

Screen reproductions in this book were created with Collage Plus from Inner Media, Inc., Hollis, NH.

Publisher: David P. Ewing

Associate Publisher: Rick Ranucci

Operations Manager: Sheila Cunningham

Publishing Plan Manager: Thomas H. Bennett

Marketing Manager: Ray Robinson

Dedication

To Mary Wing, a courageous friend. Keep the faith.

QBASIC FOR ROOKIES

Credits

Publishing Manager:
Joseph B. Wikert

Production Editor:
Jodi Jensen

Editors:
Phil Kitchel
Lori Cates

Technical Review:
Discovery Computing Inc.

Illustrator:
Gary Varvel

Book Designer:
Amy Peppler-Adams

Production Team:

Danielle Bird
Julie Brown
Jodie Cantwell
Laurie Casey
Brad Chinn
Brook Farling
Mitzi Gianakos

Michael Hughes
Heather Kaufman
Bob LaRoche
Jay Lesandrini
Caroline Roop
Linda Seifert

Composed in Goudy and MCPdigital by Que Corporation

About the Author

Clayton Walnum has been writing about computers for a decade and has published over 300 articles in major computer publications. He is the author of 10 books, covering such diverse topics as programming, computer gaming, and application programs. His most recent book is *Borland C++ Power Programming*, also published by Que. His earlier titles include *PC Picasso: A Child's Computer Drawing Kit* and *The First Book of Microsoft Works For Windows* (Sams); *PowerMonger: The Official Strategy Guide* (Prima); and *C-manship Complete* (Taylor Ridge Books). Mr. Walnum is a full-time free-lance writer and lives in Connecticut with his wife and their three children.

Acknowledgments

I would like to thank the following people for their contribution to this book: Joe Wikert for his guidance and for keeping me busy; Jodi Jensen, Phil Kitchel, and Lori Cates for combing the snarls out of the manuscript; and Discovery Computing Inc. for making sure I really did know what I was talking about. As always, a special thank you goes out to my family. Finally, a heartfelt thanks to Stu Wing for a lot of great Saturday nights. Why'd you move, buddy? We miss you already.

Trademark Acknowledgments

All terms mentioned in this book that are known to be trademarks or service marks have been appropriately capitalized. Que Corporation cannot attest to the accuracy of this information. Use of a term in this book should not be regarded as affecting the validity of any trademark or service mark.

IBM is a registered trademark of International Business Machines, Inc.

MS-DOS is a registered trademark and QBasic is a trademark of Microsoft Corporation.

Contents at a Glance

QBASIC FOR ROOKIES

Table of Contents

QBASIC FOR ROOKIES

Introduction

Have you ever wondered what goes on inside a computer program? Did you ever want to sit down at your keyboard and conjure up digital magic on your computer's screen? If so, there may be a computer programmer lurking inside you screaming to get out.

Unfortunately, you may see computer programming not only as intimidating but as downright scary. Heck, you get new gray hairs every time you try to write a simple batch file, right? If you feel this way, *QBasic for Rookies* is here to prove that programming your computer can be fun, rewarding, and—best of all—easy.

Who This Book Is For

This book is for anyone who wants to learn to program their computer using QBasic. More importantly, this book is for anyone who's flipped through other programming texts only to be discouraged by obtuse language, jargon-ridden prose, and a stuffed-shirt attitude. The conversational style you'll find in *QBasic for Rookies* incorporates plain-English explanations along with short programming examples. Together, these elements lead you (the novice programmer) by the hand through the techno-jungle of computer programming.

Because it focuses on beginning programmers, *QBasic for Rookies* is not a complete QBasic reference, nor is it a comprehensive tutorial covering the techniques of professional programming. *QBasic for Rookies* is meant to give you a quick taste of QBasic programming so that you can decide whether programming is as interesting as you thought it would be. By the end of the book, you will know all you need to know to write many fun and useful programs. After you've worked your way through this entire book, however, you'll probably want to purchase a more advanced text so that you can learn the complete QBasic language. Recommended books are provided at the end of Chapter 9.

Software and Hardware Requirements

Although QBasic runs on most IBM-compatible computers that have DOS 5.0 or later, a couple of the programs in this book require a color monitor. Even if you don't have a color monitor, you can still follow most of the lessons with little difficulty. In addition, a mouse is often helpful for selecting menus and buttons. But if you don't have a mouse, don't worry. You can control QBasic completely from the keyboard, and you can get by just fine without a mouse. Finally, you must have at least one floppy disk drive; a hard drive, however, will make your programming much more enjoyable.

As for software, you just need a copy of QBasic, which comes bundled with DOS Version 5.0 or later. The rest of the software you'll write yourself!

What's in This Book

QBasic for Rookies is composed of nine chapters, each of which concentrates on specific topics of importance to novice programmers. Here's a brief outline of the book:

▼ *Chapter 1* is an introduction to the art of programming. Here, you learn what programs are and how they work. You also learn the general programming process.

▼ *Chapter 2* teaches you how to use the QBasic programming environment. You get hands-on experience with QBasic's editor, menus, dialog boxes, and much more.

▼ *Chapter 3* covers such topics as moving data in and out of your computer and using variables. You also learn what interactive programs are and how to write them.

▼ *Chapter 4* introduces you to computer mathematics. You learn to do such things as count in a program and write simple QBasic formulas. You also get a quick look at data types.

▼ *Chapter 5* offers a discussion of text in computer programs, including using string (text) variables in conjunction with some of QBasic's most-used string-handling functions.

▼ *Chapter 6* teaches you how computers make decisions. Here, you learn about IF–THEN statements, as well as relational operators (such as greater-than, less-than, and equal-to) and logical operators (AND, OR, and NOT).

▼ *Chapter 7* introduces you to QBasic's powerful looping constructs, including FOR–NEXT, WHILE, and DO loops. You can use loops to more easily write programs that perform repetitive operations.

▼ *Chapter 8* teaches you about arrays—special data structures that can hold many values. You'll learn to create numerical and text arrays, as well as discover various ways to load values into an array.

▼ *Chapter 9* sums things up with a discussion of modular program design and using QBasic's built-in debugger to find errors in your programs.

Conventions Used in This Book

To get the most out of this book, you should know a little about how it's designed. Here are a few tips:

▼ New terms and emphasized words are presented in *italicized text*; pay close attention to these terms. QBasic programs, keywords, commands, variable names, and the like are set in a special monospace type, as in PRINT "Hello!".

▼ Anything you are asked to type appears in **bold**. Responses to program prompts appear in **monospace bold**.

▼ QBasic programs are numbered and have bold headings, such as **Listing 7.1 REPEAT.BAS prints your name six times**.

▼ Tables and figures are also numbered and help organize material within chapters.

▼ Descriptive labels, called *callouts*, appear next to some program lines. These callouts help you follow along by pointing to particular items that are being discussed in the text.

What Are Those Drawings in the Margin?

This book uses icons (those funny drawings in the margin) to say things like "Be careful when you do this," or "Here's more information about this new term." The following is an explanation of these visual pointers:

CAUTION

Beware! Warning! This icon warns you of problem areas, including possible cases in which you might introduce bugs into your program or crash your system.

NOTE

This icon points out extraneous information. Sometimes, this information helps speed your learning process and provides you with QBasic shortcuts. Other times, it simply reminds you of information important enough to be mentioned twice.

BUZZWORD

BUZZWORD

Terms you are being introduced to for the first time are indicated by this icon. Most of these terms are also italicized in text, but the Buzzword box emphasizes the importance of certain terms. Although *QBasic for Rookies* avoids computer jargon as much as possible, there are some terms that every programmer must understand.

TIP

This icon focuses your attention on suggestions that can help you program more quickly and efficiently. Some tips may help you use the QBasic programming environment more effectively. Others may provide handy programming ideas to help you write well-constructed programs.

IN SIMPLE TERMS

Detailed descriptions of how a program works are indicated by this icon. This type of box appears after nearly every program listing and supplements the explanation given in the text.

CATCH THIS!

In a few instances in this book, an important concept or idea is tagged with this icon. Be sure to read any paragraphs flagged with this little picture.

Step Into the Strange and Wonderful World of QBasic

Still with us? Good news! Just around the corner is your first QBasic programming lesson. We can stay here and chat all day, or you can turn the page and start on your fun-filled vacation in QBasicland. See you there.

CHAPTER 1

A Programming Primer

(Stepping into the Dark Unknown)

IN A NUTSHELL

▼ Exploring the reasons to program

▼ Examining the parts of a program

▼ Learning about different computer languages

▼ Writing a computer program

CHAPTER 1

Before you get started with computer programming, it might help to have a basic understanding of what it's all about. You undoubtedly have some ideas about what a program is and how it works, or you wouldn't have bought this book to begin with. Some of these ideas may be right on the money; others may be as crazy as a whale in a tutu.

Whatever your ideas about programming, this chapter gives you the skinny, the real poop, the absolute truth. After reading this chapter, you may find that your perceptions about programming are pretty solid; or you may find that you know as much about programming a computer as you do about building a submarine. In either case, you'll be a better person for having spent time here. If nothing else, you're about to learn a surprising secret—and everyone likes secrets.

The Surprising Secret

(Mum's the word)

The computer programming world has a well-kept secret. You won't hear programmers talking about it (which is, of course, why it's a secret). And if you've been using a computer for any time at all, you'll probably find this secret hard to believe. Nevertheless, it's as true as the sky is blue. So brace yourself. You're about to learn a shocking fact. Ready?

Computers are stupid.

It's true! Just how stupid are they? Computers are so stupid, they make avocados look like brain surgeons. Fact is, a computer can do absolutely nothing on its own. Without programmers, computers are as useless as rubber razors. Computers can do only what they're told to do. And if you think for a minute, you'll realize this means that computers can only

perform tasks which humans already know how to do. So why do we bother with computers? The great thing about computers is not that they're smart, but that they can perform endless calculations quickly and without getting bored.

Programmers are the people who tell computers what to do. That's not to say that when you *use* your computer you're programming it. For example, when you plop yourself down in front of a word processor and hack out a letter to Aunt Martha, you're not giving commands to the computer. You're only using the commands already contained in the program. It's the computer program—which was written by a programmer—that actually tells the computer what to do.

Fig. 1 shows the relationship between a computer user, a program, and a computer. That's you, the computer user, way up at the top of the hierarchy (feeling dizzy?). You probably use your computer for many activities besides word processing, such as organizing data in a spreadsheet, keeping track of information in a database, and maybe even for playing games. In all these cases, you execute a program, which in turn provides instructions to the computer.

The bottom line is that if you want to give commands directly to your computer, you must learn to write programs. And that's why you bought this book.

QBASIC FOR ROOKIES

Why Learn to Program?

(What's in it for me?)

There can be as many reasons for you to learn to program as there are raisins in California. Only you know what attracts you to programming. Here are some of the reasons that may be going through your mind:

▼ You're looking for a fun and rewarding hobby.

▼ You want to be able to write the programs you really need—the ones you can't always find at the software store.

▼ You want to learn more about how computers work.

▼ You have to learn programming for school or work.

▼ You want to impress your friends.

▼ Some misguided person gave you this book as a gift, and you don't want to hurt his or her feelings.

These all are legitimate reasons. You may even have a better one. Whatever your reason, once you get started with programming, you'll find it can be both fascinating and addictive. Your spouse or significant other, however, may ban computers from your home and burn this book after he or she realizes just how addictive computer programming can be. Consider yourself warned.

What's a Computer Program?

(Looks like Greek to me)

Did you ever build a model airplane? When you opened the box, you found a list of numbered instructions. By following the instructions in the order in which they were presented, you put your model together piece by piece. When you finally reached the last instruction, your model was complete—except, of course, for those few parts that are always left over.

A computer program is much like that list of instructions; the instructions in a computer program, however, don't tell *you* what to do. They tell the computer what to do.

Still, a computer program is nothing more than a list of commands. The computer follows these commands, one by one, until it reaches the end of the program. Unlike your experience with the model, however, the computer will have no leftover pieces. Computers are stupid, not sloppy.

BUZZWORD

Computer Program

A *computer program* is a list of instructions the computer follows from beginning to end. A *computer programmer* writes this list of instructions using one of the many computer languages available.

Each line in a computer program is usually a single command that the computer must obey. Each command does only a very small task, such as printing a name on the screen or adding two numbers together. When you put hundreds, thousands, or even hundreds of thousands of these commands together, your computer can do wonderful things: balance a checkbook, print a document, draw pictures, or blast invading aliens from the skies.

As you see in the next section, computer programs can be written in any one of many different languages.

Programming Languages

(*Parlez-Vous* BASIC?)

Computers don't understand English. They're stupid, remember? They can't even understand QBasic. They're *really* stupid. Computers understand only one thing, *machine language*, which is entirely composed of numbers. Unfortunately, some human minds don't deal well with numbers. Imagine, for example, a human language in which the numbers 10, 12, 14, and 15 had the following significance:

    10   hello

    12   you

    14   how

    15   are

BUZZWORD

Machine Language

Machine language is the only language your computer really understands. It consists of nothing but a bunch of numbers that are very difficult, if not impossible, for humans to understand. Programming languages like QBasic enable people to write programs in an English-like language that is then changed into machine language so the computer can understand it.

Now, imagine walking up to a friend and saying, "10, 14 15 12?" Your friend wouldn't know what to say. (If your friend answers "32 65 34," he spends way too much time with computers. Get him help.) If you expect your friend to respond, you'd better use the words "Hello, how are you?" Conversely, if we mere mortals have any hope of making sense of machine language, we have to change it into something we can understand—something that has as little to do with numbers as a vegetarian has to do with steak. That's where QBasic (or any other computer language) comes in.

QBasic programs are a dialect of a computer language called BASIC (Beginner's All-purpose Symbolic Instruction Code), which was developed not to help computers, but to help people make sense out of the numerical nonsense machines delight in. QBasic replaces many of the numbers used by machine language with words and symbols we lowly humans can more easily understand and remember.

NOTE

There are many versions of the BASIC language, of which QBasic is only one. Older versions of DOS (before Version 5.0) came with a version of BASIC called GW-BASIC. You can also go down to your local software store and buy QuickBASIC or Visual Basic. All of these software packages enable you to create computer programs with BASIC, but they all implement the BASIC language in slightly different ways.

Now, wait a minute. Computers understand only numbers, right? And a BASIC program uses words and symbols (with a few numbers) so that people can understand the program. How, then, can the computer understand and run BASIC?

The truth is, when you load QBasic, you are also loading an *interpreter*, which is a special program that can take the words and symbols from a

BASIC program and convert them into machine language that the computer can understand. Without QBasic's interpretation of your programs, your computer wouldn't have the slightest idea what to do with the program. Fig. 2 summarizes this conversion process.

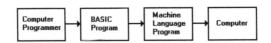

Fig. 2

Computer Programmer → BASIC Program → Machine Language Program → Computer

BUZZWORD

BASIC Interpreter

A *BASIC interpreter* is a program that changes BASIC programs into machine language that the computer can understand.

Many different kinds of computer languages exist, including Pascal, C++, FORTRAN, COBOL, Modula-2, and BASIC. All computer languages have one thing in common: they can be read by humans and, therefore, must be converted to machine language before the computer can understand them.

Some languages, such as BASIC, convert the program to machine language one line at a time as the program runs. Other languages, such as Pascal, use a *compiler* to convert the entire program all at once before any of the program begins executing. All programming languages *must* be converted to machine language in order for the computer to understand the program's instructions.

BUZZWORD

Compiler and Executable File

A *compiler* changes your program into an *executable file* (for example, WORD.EXE or SIMCITY.EXE) that can be run from the DOS prompt. An executable program is actually a machine language program that's ready for your computer to read and understand. With a few exceptions, most computer programming languages are distributed with a compiler.

Because QBasic uses an interpreter to translate your program into machine language as the program runs, you cannot run a QBasic program from the DOS prompt. To run a QBasic program, you must first load the program into the QBasic interpreter and then select the interpreter's RUN command. Many modern versions of BASIC, however, now use compilers to change BASIC programs into executable files, which can be run from the DOS prompt. QuickBASIC, the commercial version of QBasic, is a compiled language and can be purchased at your local software store.

The Programming Process

(Getting down to the nitty-gritty)

Now that you know something about computer programs, how do you go about creating one? Writing a computer program, although not particularly difficult, can be a long and tedious process. It's much like writing a term paper for school or a financial report for your boss. You start out with a basic idea of what you want to do, and you write a first draft. After reading over the draft and resisting the urge to throw the pages into the fireplace, you go back to writing—polishing your prose until it glows like a gem in the sun. Over the course of the writing process, you may write many drafts before you're satisfied with the document you've produced.

QBASIC FOR ROOKIES

Writing a QBasic program requires development steps similar to those you use when you write a paper or report. The following list outlines these steps:

1. Type the program using QBasic's editor.

2. Save the program to disk.

3. Run the program and see how it works.

4. Fix programming errors.

5. Go back to Step 2.

As you can see, most of the steps in the programming process are performed over and over again as errors are discovered and corrected. Even experienced programmers seldom write programs that are error-free. Programmers spend more time fine-tuning their programs than they do writing them initially, which is why they eat so many Gummy Bears and drink so much Coke. All that rewriting saps their energy and lowers their blood-sugar levels.

This fine-tuning is important because we humans are not as logical as we like to think. Moreover, our minds are incapable of remembering every detail required to make a program run perfectly. Heck, most of us are lucky if we can remember our telephone numbers. Only when a program crashes or does something else unexpected can we hope to find those sneaky errors that hide in programs. Computer experts say that there's no such thing as a bug-free program. After you start writing full-length programs, you'll see how true this statement is.

PLAY BALL!

BUZZWORD

Bugs

Bugs are programming errors that stop your program from running correctly. Bugs are also nasty creatures with spindly legs and crunchy shells that make you scream when they leap out of shadows. But this book doesn't deal with that kind of bug, so we won't talk about them anymore.

Is Programming Easy?

(Squashing that panic attack)

After reading all that's involved in writing and running a computer program, you might be a little nervous. After all, you bought this book because it promised to teach you computer programming. No one warned you about such mysterious topics as machine language, interpreters, compilers, and program bugs. So, is programming easy or not?

Well, yes and no.

It's easy to learn to write simple programs with QBasic. The QBasic language is logical, English-like, and easy to understand. With only minimal practice, you can write many useful and fun programs with QBasic. All you need is the time to read this book and the ambition to write a few programs of your own. In fact, what you'll learn in this book is enough programming for just about anyone who's not planning to be a professional programmer.

However, if you want to make programming a career, you have much to learn that's not covered in this introductory book. For example, consider a word-processing program like Microsoft Word, which took dozens of programmers many years to write. To write such complex software, you

must have intimate knowledge of how your computer works. Additionally, you must have spent many years learning the ins and outs of professional computer programming.

Still, there's a lot you can do with QBasic, whether you're interested in writing utilities, simple applications, or even games. And, once you get the hang of it, you'll discover that programming in BASIC is not as difficult as you may have thought.

After all, computers may be stupid, but you're not.

Summing Up

▼ A computer can do only what a human instructs it to do.

▼ There are many reasons to learn to program, but, if nothing else, programming is a satisfying hobby.

▼ A computer program is a list of commands that the computer follows from beginning to end.

▼ There are many computer languages. The language you learn in this book is called BASIC.

▼ A BASIC program must be converted to machine language before the computer can understand it. This conversion is done by QBasic's interpreter.

▼ Writing a program is a lot like writing a text document. You must write several "drafts" before the program is complete.

▼ Programming with QBasic is as easy or difficult as you want it to be.

Now that you know what computer programming is, it's time to learn how to use QBasic's program editor—which is where you'll be spending a lot of time over the course of this book. In the next chapter, you not only learn how to use the QBasic programming environment, but you write your first QBasic program.

CHAPTER 2
Welcome to QBasic
(Let the Fun Begin)

IN A NUTSHELL

- ▼ Running QBasic
- ▼ Giving commands to QBasic
- ▼ Loading, saving, and printing programs
- ▼ Typing program text
- ▼ Editing program text
- ▼ Finding words or phrases in a program

Now that you have a general idea of what a computer program is and how it works, it's time to load up QBasic and get to work. In this chapter, you learn about the QBasic programming environment and write your first program. If you've used word processors before, this chapter covers a lot of familiar ground. If you have no experience with text editing, however, you should study carefully the discussions that follow. After all, you can't write a program until you know how to type it in!

Where Is QBasic?

(Diving into DOS)

As you may already know, your computer's operating system is called MS-DOS, which stands for Most Skunks Don Oval Slippers. (If you believe that, you might want to explore other career opportunities.) Actually, MS-DOS stands for Microsoft Disk Operating System. This operating system, just like any other program, is software that was installed on your computer. It may already have been installed when you bought your computer, or you may have installed it yourself. In either case, you should have a directory on your hard disk named DOS, which is where DOS lives.

BUZZWORD

> **MS-DOS**
>
> Your computer's operating system is named MS-DOS, which stands for Microsoft Disk Operating System. Called DOS for short, this operating system is loaded into your computer's memory when you turn on your computer. Without DOS loaded, your computer will do nothing but sit uselessly on your desk.

If you look in the DOS directory, you'll find almost 100 files. Most of these files make up the MS-DOS operating system and the commands that you can type from your computer's prompt. In order to be a programmer, you must memorize all the file names in the DOS directory and be prepared to recite them in alphabetical order. (Just kidding.)

Some files in the DOS directory have little to do with DOS. One of these files, QBASIC.EXE, is the QBasic programming language, which comes free with MS-DOS Version 5.0 and later. Besides QBASIC.EXE, there are a few other files that work with QBasic. One is QBASIC.HLP, which is QBasic's help file. Other files are sample QBasic programs and have a .BAS file name extension. These sample programs include GORILLAS.BAS, MONEY.BAS, NIBBLES.BAS, and REMLINE.BAS. (Unfortunately, Microsoft decided not to include these sample programs with MS-DOS 6.0. You can, however, still get these files by ordering a supplemental disk from Microsoft. Refer to your MS-DOS 6 documentation for instructions on ordering this disk.)

If you plan to do a lot of QBasic programming, you might want to move all QBasic-related files into a separate directory, away from all the crowding and confusion of the DOS directory. To do this, follow these instructions:

1. At your computer's DOS prompt, type **CD ** and press Enter. This command ensures that you are logged into your hard disk's root (main) directory, not some other directory.

2. Type **MD QBASIC** and press Enter. This command creates a new directory called QBASIC.

3. Type **CD DOS** and press Enter. This command moves you into the DOS directory, where the QBasic files are located.

4. Type **COPY QBASIC.* C:\QBASIC** and press Enter. This command copies all files starting with "QBASIC" to your new QBASIC directory. These files are QBASIC.EXE and QBASIC.HLP.

5. Type **COPY *.BAS C:\QBASIC** and press Enter. This command copies all QBASIC sample programs to your new directory. These programs are GORILLAS.BAS, MONEY.BAS, NIBBLES.BAS, and REMLINE.BAS. (If you have MS-DOS 6, you should skip this step and instead order the supplemental disk from Microsoft, which contains the sample QBasic programs. For the rest of this chapter, we assume that you have obtained these sample programs and have copied them to your QBasic directory.)

All QBasic-related files are now in your new QBASIC directory. To find those files from your hard drive's root directory, type **CD QBASIC**. You can get to the QBASIC directory from any other directory by typing the full path name for the directory: **CD C:\QBASIC**. Alternatively, if you have a particularly vivid imagination, you can get to the directory by having Scotty beam you there.

After changing to the QBASIC directory, you can type the command **DIR** to see all the files stored there. Currently, you'll see only those files you just copied. However, after you do some programming, you'll see your own programs there too (unless, of course, you move them to another directory).

Loading QBasic

(Every journey starts with the first step)

Before you can run a QBasic program or write programs of your own, you must load QBasic. This is no different from having to load a word

processor before writing a document—except with QBasic, you'll never feel obligated to write a letter to weird Uncle Henry. QBasic actually includes its own word processing program, which you use to write your programs. To load QBasic, switch to the QBASIC directory, type **QBASIC**, and press Enter. When you do, you'll see a screen similar to the one in Fig. 1.

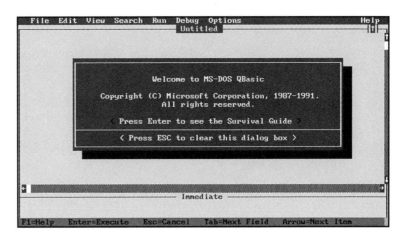

The welcome dialog box enables you to look at QBasic's Survival Guide (a brief help screen) by pressing Enter or by using your mouse to click on the `Press Enter to see the Survival Guide` text line. To get rid of the dialog box and get started with QBasic, press your keyboard's Esc key or use your mouse to click on the `Press ESC to clear this dialog box` text line.

When you close the welcome dialog box, you'll see QBasic's main window, as shown in Fig. 2.

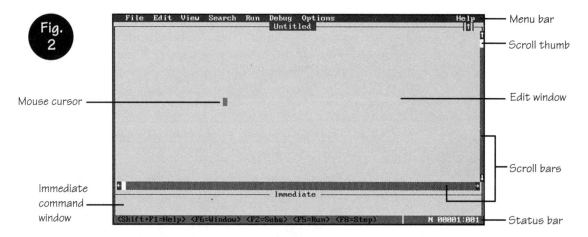

Fig. 2

Menu bar
Scroll thumb
Edit window
Scroll bars
Status bar

Mouse cursor

Immediate command window

QBasic's main window is composed of a couple of smaller windows and bars, each labeled in Fig. 2 and listed here:

Menu bar: You can access QBasic's various commands from here.

Edit window: You type and view your programs in this window.

Immediate command window: Any programming commands you type in this window are performed immediately by the computer, rather than added to your program. You'll learn about immediate commands later in this book. However, you might as well know now that commands like "Get me a date with Michelle Pfeiffer" don't work worth a darn.

Status bar: The status bar shows the keys you can press to access certain commands and gives a quick description of any highlighted menu command. It also shows the line and column position of the text cursor.

Now that you know how the QBasic main screen is set up, let's take a closer look at this powerful programming environment.

Using QBasic's Menu Bar

(A look at today's specials)

Computers are stupid, and so is QBasic. You can sit at your desk and stare at QBasic's main screen as long as you like, but until you give it a command, it'll just sit and stare back. Worse, you'll always be the first to blink.

As in many computer programs, you can use your keyboard or your mouse to give commands to QBasic by selecting entries from the menu bar at the top of the screen. To select commands with your keyboard, first tap the Alt key. Notice that the first letter of each menu title lights up, and a black box appears around the File menu title. The black box indicates the menu that will open when you press Enter.

To select the menu you want, use the left and right arrows to move the black box. When the black box is on the menu you want, press Enter to open that menu.

TIP

You can open any menu instantly by holding down the Alt key and pressing the first letter of the menu's title. For example, to open the File menu, press Alt-F. The letter F is called a shortcut key. The shortcut key is not always the first letter of the menu or option.

When the menu appears, use the up- and down-arrow keys to highlight the command you want. Press Enter to activate the highlighted command.

Using a mouse to select menu commands is a little easier. Place the mouse pointer over the menu title and click the left mouse button. When the menu drops down, click on the command you want to issue.

Don't fret about what all the menu commands do. You'll learn most of them later. For now, how about using the **F**ile menu to have a little fun?

Loading a QBasic Program

(Lights, camera, action!)

Before you can run a QBasic program, the program must be loaded. This doesn't mean that you should force your program to chugalug a quart of Smirnoff's; it means that you must bring the program's text file (called the *source code*) into QBasic's editor window. You do this with the Open... command from the File menu, which is shown in Fig. 3.

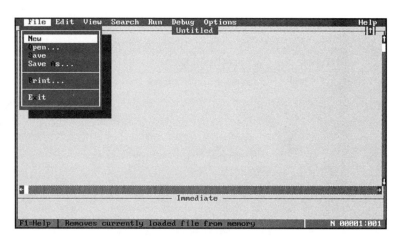

When you select the Open... command, you'll see a dialog box similar to the one shown in Fig. 4.

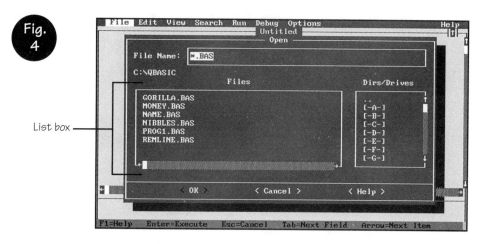

Fig. 4

List box

Source Code

PLAY BALL!

BUZZWORD

Source code is the program text that you type into an editor. To run a program with QBasic, you must first load your source code into the QBasic editor. With compiled languages, a program's source code is no longer needed after the program is compiled. Still, programmers usually save their source code so that they can make changes or additions to the program. Programmers also save their source code so that they can impress friends and attract members of the opposite sex with their cleverness.

As with menus, you can use either your keyboard or mouse to select files from the dialog box shown in Fig.4. To use your keyboard, type the name of the file you want to load and press Enter. If you want to avoid typing the file name, press Tab to move the cursor to the Files list box. Use the up- and down-arrow keys to highlight the appropriate file, and press Enter to load the file.

PLAY BALL!

BUZZWORD

Tabbing

Tabbing is the process of using your computer's Tab key to move from one part of a dialog box to another. Most dialog boxes contain various components, such as text-entry fields and buttons, which you can access in a couple of different ways. If you have a mouse, you can click on the field or button you want to access. Keyboard users can tap the Tab key to move to the next field or button in the dialog box. When you reach the last field or button, pressing Tab again returns you to the first field or button.

You can select any button at the bottom of the dialog box by pressing your keyboard's Tab key until the blinking text cursor is on the button. Then press Enter.

To select a file using your mouse, *double-click* the file in the Files list box. (To double-click is to place your mouse pointer over the item and click the left mouse button twice in rapid succession.) You can also select the file by clicking the file once to highlight it and then clicking the OK button at the bottom of the dialog box.

If you change your mind about opening a file, just select the Cancel button.

Try opening the sample program named NIBBLES.BAS. After opening this file, your screen should look something like Fig. 5. If your screen doesn't look like this figure, you've either opened the wrong file or you're overdue for an eye examination.

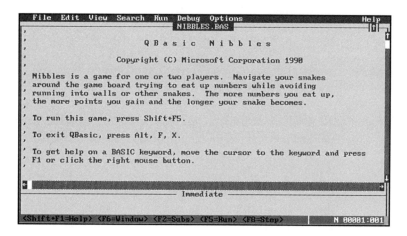

Fig.
5

Nibbles is a simple game in which you control a snake named Sammy. Your task is to guide Sammy around the screen (using the arrow keys) so that he can gobble up the numbers that appear on the playfield. When Sammy eats a number, he grows longer. The longer he gets, the harder he is to control. Whatever you do, be sure that Sammy doesn't collide with himself or any of the playfield's walls.

Go ahead and give Nibbles a shot. To run the program, select the Start command from the Run menu, or simply press Shift-F5. You can stop the program at any time by pressing Ctrl-Break on your keyboard. This program gives you a small dose of the neat stuff you can do with QBasic, so have a ball. After playing Nibbles, drop in again at the next section.

Controlling the Edit Window

(Arrows, scrollers, and cursors, oh my!)

By now, you've probably noticed that QBasic's edit window has a couple of extra controls. Along the right side and bottom of the window are

scroll bars that allow you to view the parts of a program that are off-screen. You can scroll the program up or down one line at a time in the edit window by using your mouse to click on the scroll bar's up or down arrows. Likewise, you can scroll left or right one character at a time by clicking on the horizontal scroll bar's arrows.

To scroll up or down a full page, click in the vertical scroll bar above or below the *scroll thumb* (the little box inside the scroll bar). Scrolling horizontally works the same way, except you click in the horizontal scroll bar. Finally, you can move instantly to any place in a program by placing your mouse cursor over the appropriate scroll thumb, holding down the left mouse button, and moving the scroll thumb to the position you want.

To scroll a program from the keyboard, use the keyboard's arrow keys or the Page Up and Page Down keys.

Typing Programs

(The pitter-patter of little keys)

Running the programs that came with your copy of QBasic is fun, but learning to play the games isn't why you're reading this book. You're reading this book either because you want to learn to program, or because somebody is reading your copy of *People*. In any case, to write QBasic programs you have to learn to use the QBasic editor. This section teaches you just that.

To start a new program, you must have an empty edit window. To open one, select the **N**ew command from the **F**ile menu, which opens an empty window named Untitled. It is into this window that you'll type the commands that make up your QBasic program. Before typing a new program, however, you should give the empty window an appropriate name. (Names like Adrian, Samantha, and Guido the Man are out.) To

name your program, first select the Save **A**s... command from the **File** menu. You'll then see a dialog box similar to the one shown in Fig. 6.

Fig. 6

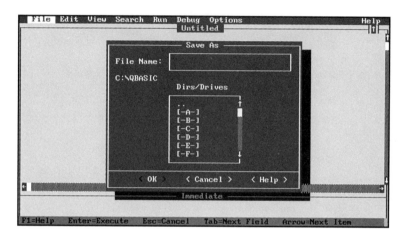

When the Save As dialog box appears, type the file name **PROG1.BAS** into the File Name edit box. Then press Enter on your keyboard or click the dialog's OK button with your mouse. The name of the Window changes to PROG1.BAS.

NOTE

> All your BASIC programs should use the file extension .BAS (Short for BASIC—get it?) because that's the extension QBasic expects programs to have. Moreover, that's the extension used by other programmers.

Now that you have a newly named program window, you can type your program. Type the letters **cls** (note the lowercase), and press Enter. What happened? If you typed the letters correctly, QBasic changed them from lowercase to uppercase. This is because CLS is a QBasic *keyword*, a word that is part of the QBasic language. (For those who are curious, CLS is the command to clear the screen. It is not, as has been rumored, the

initials of the guy who discovered Marshmallow Fluff.) Whenever
QBasic recognizes a keyword, it automatically makes it all capital letters.

Keyword

A *keyword* is a word that is part of a programming language.
Keywords, also known as *reserved words*, cannot be used as
names for anything else in a program.

Now type the following text line, exactly as it is here. Make sure you
include all punctuation (and the misspelled words!):

```
input Whatis yourr name"; Name$
```

When you press Enter, you see a dialog box similar to the one shown in
Fig. 7. This is a syntax error dialog box—QBasic's way of telling you that
you're not as smart as you think you are. Just as with human languages,
such as English, computer languages have rules that dictate how sentences (or, in this case, commands) must be constructed. In the line you
just typed, you didn't follow the rules, so QBasic complained.

Fig. 7

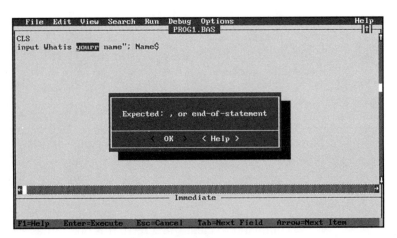

To fix the line so QBasic can understand it, you must add a quotation mark immediately before the word What. First, press Enter to get rid of the syntax error dialog box. Next, use the left-arrow key to move the flashing text cursor under the letter W in the word What. Finally, type a quotation mark (") and press the down-arrow key to move to the next line.

Now QBasic recognizes the command. In addition, it changed the word input to all capital letters because INPUT, like CLS, is a QBasic keyword. However, just because QBasic can now make sense of the line doesn't mean the line is correct. It only means that the line follows QBasic's syntax rules. You still have two misspelled words: yourr and Whatis.

QBasic's text editor lets you easily correct typing mistakes. First, use the arrow keys to position the flashing text cursor under the space between the words yourr and name. Now, press the Backspace key. Presto! The extra letter vanishes, and the rest of the line moves to the left to fill in the space you deleted.

You still have a mistake in the line, though. There should be a space between the words What and is. Luckily, you can add characters to a line as easily as you can delete them. Use the arrow keys to position the blinking text cursor under the i in the word Whatis, and then press the space bar. When you do, a space character appears at the text cursor's position and the rest of the line moves to the right.

Finish typing the program by adding the lines that follow this paragraph. Remember to type them exactly as they're shown. To indent the line that begins with the word PRINT, press the space bar two times.

```
FOR X = 1 TO 200
  PRINT Name$; " ";
NEXT X
```

Your screen should now resemble Fig. 8.

Fig.
8

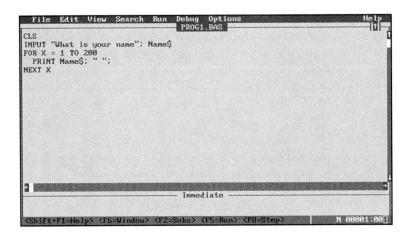

```
 File  Edit  View  Search  Run  Debug  Options                    Help
                          PROG1.BAS
CLS
INPUT "What is your name"; Name$
FOR X = 1 TO 200
  PRINT Name$; " ";
NEXT X




                            Immediate
<Shift+F1=Help> <F6=Window> <F2=Subs> <F5=Run> <F8=Step>      N 00001:001
```

Soon you'll run the program and see what it does. First you should save
your program to disk. Then, if anything goes wrong when you run it, you
won't lose your work. (It's possible for a programming error to lock up
your computer, forcing you to restart it. It's also possible for a programming error to infuriate you enough that you throw your computer out
the nearest window. In either case, you'll be glad you saved your program
first.)

To save your program, select the **S**ave command from the **F**ile menu.
After you select this command, your program is safely stored on your disk
under the name PROG1.BAS (or whatever you named the program).

To run the program, select the **S**tart command from the **R**un menu, or
press Shift-F5. This program first asks you to enter your name. Type your
name and press Enter. You should then see a screen similar to Fig. 9. To
get back to QBasic, press any key—as it says at the bottom of the screen.

Congratulations! You've just written and run your first QBasic program.
Pat yourself on the back, go get a snack, and brag until everyone in your
household is thoroughly annoyed.

Fig. 9

```
What is your name? Henry
Henry Henry Henry Henry Henry Henry Henry Henry Henry Henry Henry Henry Henry
Henry Henry Henry Henry Henry Henry Henry Henry Henry Henry Henry Henry Henry
Henry Henry Henry Henry Henry Henry Henry Henry Henry Henry Henry Henry Henry
Henry Henry Henry Henry Henry Henry Henry Henry Henry Henry Henry Henry Henry
Henry Henry Henry Henry Henry Henry Henry Henry Henry Henry Henry Henry Henry
Henry Henry Henry Henry Henry Henry Henry Henry Henry Henry Henry Henry Henry
Henry Henry Henry Henry Henry Henry Henry Henry Henry Henry Henry Henry Henry
Henry Henry Henry Henry Henry Henry Henry Henry Henry Henry Henry Henry Henry
Henry Henry Henry Henry Henry Henry Henry Henry Henry Henry Henry Henry Henry
Henry Henry Henry Henry Henry Henry Henry Henry Henry Henry Henry Henry Henry
Henry Henry Henry Henry Henry Henry Henry Henry Henry Henry Henry Henry Henry
Henry Henry Henry Henry Henry Henry Henry Henry Henry Henry Henry Henry Henry
Henry Henry Henry Henry Henry Henry Henry Henry Henry Henry Henry Henry Henry
Henry Henry Henry Henry Henry Henry Henry Henry Henry Henry Henry Henry Henry
Henry Henry Henry Henry Henry Henry Henry Henry Henry Henry Henry Henry Henry
Henry Henry Henry Henry Henry



Press any key to continue
```

Printing a Program

(A masterpiece suitable for framing)

If you have a printer connected to your system, you can print a hard
copy of your program. Although you don't have to print your programs,
you might want to have a copy on paper to file away. Also, it's often
easier to find programming errors on paper than on-screen. More importantly, printing programs uses up ink and paper, which makes it look like
you're actually accomplishing something. (Of course, wasting paper also
kills trees, so you might want to examine your priorities.)

How about printing the program you just wrote? To print, select the
Print... command from the **F**ile menu. You'll see a dialog box similar to
the one shown in Fig. 10.

The Print dialog box contains several printing options. You can print
selected text only (you'll learn to select text later in this chapter), text
shown in the current window only, or the entire program.

Fig.
10

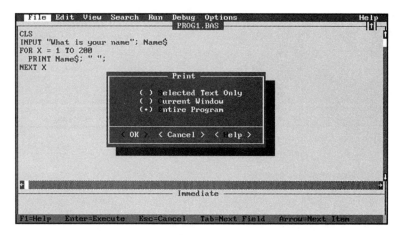

```
 File  Edit  View  Search  Run  Debug  Options                    Help
                        PROG1.BAS
CLS
INPUT "What is your name"; Name$
FOR X = 1 TO 200
   PRINT Name$; " ";
NEXT X
                        ┌──────── Print ────────┐
                        │                        │
                        │  ( ) Selected Text Only│
                        │  ( ) Current Window    │
                        │  (•) Entire Program    │
                        │                        │
                        │ < OK >  < Cancel >  < Help > │
                        └────────────────────────┘



                           Immediate
 F1=Help   Enter=Execute   Esc=Cancel   Tab=Next Field   Arrow=Next Item
```

When the Print dialog box first appears, it assumes that you want to print the entire program, so that option is already selected for you. (Nothing like a mind-reading computer, eh?) However, you can change the option easily. From your keyboard, use the up and down arrows to move the selection marker (the dot) to the option you want, and then press Enter. To use your mouse, click on the option you want and then click on the OK button.

PLAY BALL!

BUZZWORD

Buttons

On-screen *buttons* are used in many computer programs and enable you to make selections in dialog boxes. Buttons in computer programs work much like buttons on machines in other areas of your life. The difference between the two is that you push an on-screen button by clicking your mouse; you push real buttons with your finger. (Some of today's computers do allow you to push on-screen buttons with your finger. In the future, most computers will work this way.) QBasic buttons usually appear at the bottom of a dialog box and are represented by a pair of angle brackets containing commands like OK or Cancel.

For now, select the Entire Program option and press Enter. The Print dialog box vanishes from the screen, and your program prints on your printer. You now can annoy people further with your bragging—they'll especially enjoy having you wave the newly printed program in their faces.

TIP

QBasic includes a sophisticated on-line help system. If you aren't sure how to do something, check the **Help** menu. This menu provides access not only to help for QBasic, but also to full instructions for using the help system. To see these instructions, select the Using **Help** command from the **Help** menu or press Shift-F1. Many dialog boxes contain a Help button that lets you get instant help about the dialog box.

Cutting, Copying, and Pasting

(Kindergarten for programmers)

Every text editor worthy of the name allows you to select text blocks and manipulate them in various ways. Never one to be left in the dirt, QBasic's editor provides you with these handy functions. You can find the text-editing functions in the **Edit** menu, shown in Fig. 11. Notice that the Cut, Copy, Paste, and Clear commands are *dimmed* (they appear in a light gray color on the menu). Being dimmed means that they aren't currently available for use. In order for these particular text-editing commands to be available, you must first have some text highlighted.

Before you can use editing functions, you must select the text those functions will manipulate. (Fig. 12 shows what a selected block of text looks like.) As with most functions, you can select text using either your keyboard or your mouse. (You can also select text by pointing to it with your little finger and saying "Select this text," followed immediately by the magic words "Please," "Thank you," and "Shala-bama-dingo." Unfortunately, this latter method rarely works.)

Fig.
11

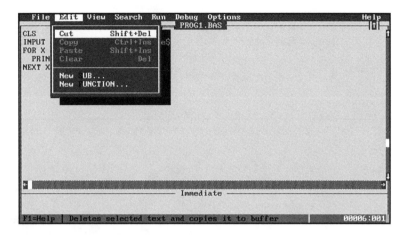

PLAY BALL!

BUZZWORD

Hot Keys

You can use hot keys to select menu commands instantly from the keyboard without first accessing the appropriate menu. For example, to cut a block of text from your program, you can access the Cut command from the **E**dit menu by simply pressing Shift-Del. You don't first have to pull down the **E**dit menu. To Paste the block of text that you cut back into your program, you can press Shift-Ins. After you learn these hot keys, you can select editing functions quickly and conveniently; unfortunately, not every menu command has a hot key.

To select text from the keyboard, first use the arrow keys to place the blinking text cursor anywhere on the first line of the text block. Then, hold down the Shift key and press the down-arrow key to highlight the lines in the block. Each time you press the down arrow, you highlight another line of text.

To select text with your mouse, place the mouse pointer on the first line you want to select, hold down the left mouse button, and drag the mouse pointer to the last line in the block.

Try selecting some text now. Using either the keyboard or mouse technique, select the middle three lines of your program's text, as shown in
Fig. 12.

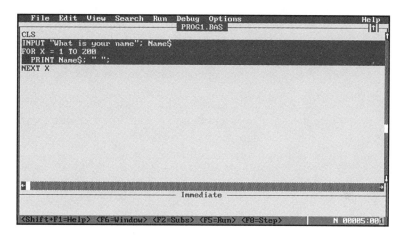

After you have selected some text, open the Edit menu. The Cut, Copy, and
Clear menu commands are now accessible. The Cut command removes the
highlighted text from the screen and places it into QBasic's clipboard (a
special text buffer from which you can later paste the text back into a different location in your program). The Copy command also places the selected
text into the clipboard, but it does so without removing the text from the
screen. Finally, the Clear command removes the selected text from the
screen, but does not place it into the clipboard.

CAUTION

When you select the Clear command from the Edit menu, any
text you have highlighted is deleted forever—so use this
command with care.

For now, select the Copy command. When you do, the Edit menu closes,
and you're back at QBasic's edit window. Everything looks the same, except
a copy of the highlighted text is now stored in QBasic's clipboard.

To use the clipboard, first deselect the selected text block by pressing any arrow key on your keyboard or by clicking your left mouse button. (Actually, you should click the left mouse button on your *mouse*. If *you* have a left mouse button, consult a surgeon immediately and have it removed.) Look at the **E**dit menu again. Because there is no longer a text block selected, the Cut, Copy, and Clear entries are no longer accessible. However, the **P**aste command is accessible. This tells you that there is text in the clipboard. In this case, it's the text you just copied.

Close the **E**dit menu, place the blinking text cursor on the first blank line below your program, and select the paste command. The text you copied is pasted into your program at the text cursor's location. Your screen should now resemble Fig. 13.

Fig. 13

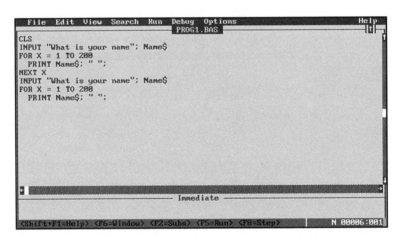

TIP

If you select the **P**aste command when you have a text block highlighted on-screen, the text in the clipboard replaces the highlighted text. Similarly, if you start typing when you have a text block highlighted, whatever you type replaces the highlighted text.

Before moving on to the next section, restore your program to its original state; you can do this either by deleting the extra lines you just pasted into it or by reloading the PROG1.BAS file. To delete a line, place the text cursor on the line and press Ctrl-Y.

Searching and Replacing

(The lost and found department)

In a small program like the one you just wrote, it's easy to find specific words or phrases. For example, if you want to find the keyword INPUT, just look at the screen and there it is. However, in large programs, finding text visually is tougher than chasing an angry bear up a tree. Luckily, QBasic includes search commands. These commands are, of course, found in the Search menu, which is shown in Fig. 14.

Fig. 14

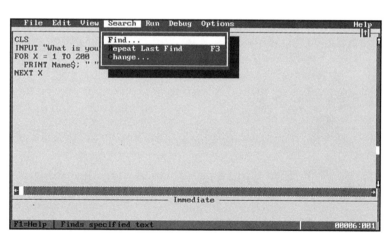

As you can see, the Search menu contains three entries: **Find...**, **Repeat Last Find**, and **Change....** To find the next occurrence (starting at the

43

text cursor's location) of any word or phrase, select the **Find...** command from the Search menu. You'll see a dialog box similar to the one shown in Fig. 15.

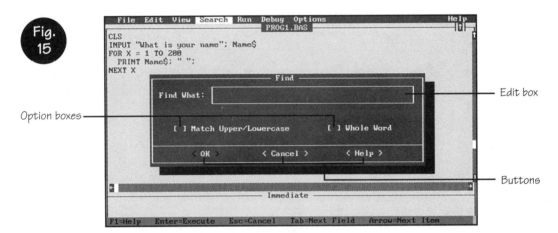

Option boxes

Edit box

Buttons

When the Find dialog box appears, the word at the text cursor's location appears in the Find What edit box. If this is the word you want to find, just press Enter to start the search. If you want to look for a different word or phrase, type it into the Find What edit box and press Enter. If you don't want to search for a word or phrase, you might want to ask yourself why the heck you're staring at the Find dialog box.

Try the Find command now by following these steps:

1. Press Ctrl-Home to place the blinking text cursor at the beginning of your program.

2. Select the **Find...** command from the Search menu. The Find dialog box appears.

3. In the Find What edit box, type the word **name** and press Enter. QBasic finds and highlights the first occurrence of the word *name*.

4. To find other occurrences of this word, select the **R**epeat Last Find command from the **S**earch menu, or just press F3. Each time you select this command, QBasic finds another occurrence of the word *name*.

Notice that QBasic doesn't care whether the word or phrase contains upper- or lowercase letters. (QBasic doesn't care that Fig Newtons have almost twice the calories of Oreos either, but that's a story for another day.) Any match is okay. You can make the search case-sensitive by checking the Match Upper/Lowercase *option box*. Option boxes look like a pair of square brackets, and you use them to turn various options on or off. When the Match Upper/Lowercase option is selected, the search finds only words that match exactly, including the case of the letters.

To select an option box from the keyboard, tab to the option box and press the space bar to toggle the option on or off. To toggle an option box with your mouse, place your mouse pointer over the option and click the left mouse button.

In addition to checking for case, you can also tell QBasic's search function to find only whole words. For example, suppose you're looking for the word "red" in your program. You select the Find function, type **red**, and press Enter. To your surprise, the first word the computer finds is `Fred` because the word `red` is part of `Fred`. If you want to find only the complete word `red`, you must check the Whole Word option box. Then the search function will ignore words that only happen to contain the letters *r-e-d*.

Now, suppose you've completed a program, and for some reason you've decided that you want to change all occurrences of the word *Name* to *FirstName*. You could go through the entire program, line-by-line, and change each occurrence of the word yourself. However, in a large program, this task would take a lot of time. Worse, you're almost certain

to miss some occurrences of the word you want to change. A better way
to tackle this problem is to use the Search menu's **Change...** command.
When you select this command, you see a dialog box similar to the one
shown in Fig. 16.

Fig.
16

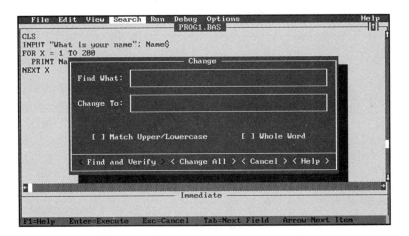

The Change dialog box looks much like the Find dialog box, except it
has two *edit boxes*—boxes into which you can type text—instead of one,
and it has different buttons at the bottom. To use the **Change** function,
type the word you want to find into the Find What edit box. Then press
Tab to move the text cursor to the Change To edit box and type the
replacement text.

You then must select one of the buttons at the bottom of the dialog box.
If you select the Find and Verify button, each time QBasic finds the
target text it'll ask whether you want to change it. If you select the
Change All button, QBasic makes all the changes without further input
from you. Using the Find and Verify button is often the best way to perform this type of global change—it ensures that only the words you want
to change get changed.

To get a little experience with the change function, use it to change all occurrences of Name in your program to FirstName. If you need help, you can follow the numbered steps below:

1. Select the **Change...** command from the Search menu. The Change dialog box appears.

2. Type the word **Name** into the Find What edit box.

3. Press the Tab key. The text cursor moves to the Change To edit box.

4. Type the word **FirstName**.

5. Press Tab. The text cursor moves to the Match Upper/Lowercase option box.

6. Press your space bar to select the Match Upper/Lowercase option.

7. Press Tab until the text cursor is on the Change All button.

8. Press Enter to select the Change All button and change all occurrences of Name to FirstName. A box appears containing the message Change complete.

9. Press Enter to remove the message box.

After you complete this change, your program should still run properly—for reasons you won't understand until later in this book. But, even if you don't understand it just now, go ahead and run the program by pressing Shift-F5. Cool, huh?

Summing Up

▼ The QBasic programming language is usually found in your DOS directory, but you can move it to its own directory if you like.

▼ To run QBasic, change to the directory that contains QBASIC.EXE and type **QBASIC**.

▼ To load a program file, select the **O**pen... command from the **F**ile menu.

▼ To save a program file to disk, use the **S**ave... or Save **A**s... command from the **F**ile menu.

▼ To start a new program, select the **N**ew command from the **F**ile menu.

▼ To print a program, select the **P**rint command from the **F**ile menu.

▼ You can view off-screen portions of a program by using the edit window's scroll bars. From your keyboard, you can scroll a program with the Page Up, Page Down, and arrow keys.

▼ QBasic changes all keywords to uppercase, regardless of how you type them. Keywords are the reserved words that make up a computer language.

▼ QBasic can find syntax errors and warn you about them. However, it can't find all possible errors in your program.

▼ To run a program, select the **S**tart command from the **R**un menu, or press Shift-F5 on your keyboard.

▼ Using the QBasic editor, you can cut, copy, and paste text much like you would with a text editor. These editing commands are located in the Edit menu, but you can also select them by using hot keys.

▼ The QBasic editor lets you find and replace words or phrases in your programs. The find and replace commands are in the Search menu.

▼ To exit QBasic, select the Exit command from the File menu.

You're now ready to move on to Chapter 3, where you'll really start learning about QBasic programming. If you'd like to take a break, you can exit QBasic by selecting the Exit command from the File menu. But, if you want to continue, follow me around the corner to the next chapter.

CHAPTER 3

Communicating with QBasic

(A Matter of Input and Output)

IN A NUTSHELL

▼ Understanding input and output

▼ Learning to use the PRINT and LPRINT commands

▼ Understanding variables

▼ Using the INPUT command

▼ Having fun with the BEEP and COLOR commands

QBASIC FOR ROOKIES

A computer wouldn't be much use if you didn't have a way of getting data in and out of it. To understand computer input and output, let's say you want to type a letter to weird Uncle Henry. Your first task is to get the characters that make up the letter into your computer's memory where you can manipulate them. You can't just dictate the letter as you would to a secretary. Computers have really terrible ears. You have to use one of the computer's input devices—in this case, the keyboard—to type your letter, placing it in memory one character at a time.

When you finish typing and editing your letter, you need a way to get it out of the computer's memory so that Uncle Henry can read it. You could call Uncle Henry and have him fly in and read the letter on your computer screen, but that kind of defeats the purpose of writing a letter. Besides, Uncle Henry hates to fly, remember? You need another kind of device—an output device—to which you can send the letter to get it into a form that is useful. You probably want to use a printer, but you could also save your letter onto a disk and send the disk to Uncle Henry. Then he could just load the letter into his computer's memory and read it on-screen.

The process of moving data in and out of a computer is called, appropriately, *input* and *output* (or I/O, for short). There are all kinds of input and output, but you only have to know about a couple to get started with QBasic. In this chapter, you'll learn to ask a user for data and accept that data from the keyboard. You'll also learn to print the data on your computer's screen or on your printer.

BUZZWORD

Input and Output Devices

Input devices, such as your keyboard and your mouse, transfer data from you to your computer. *Output devices,* such as printers and monitors, transfer data from the computer back to you. Some devices, such as disk drives, are both input and output devices.

QBASIC FOR ROOKIES

Computer Programs and I/O

(Who's the boss?)

Most input and output is controlled by the program that is currently running. If you load a program that doesn't use the keyboard, the program will not notice your keystrokes—no matter how much you type. Likewise, if a program wasn't designed to use your printer, you have no way of accessing the printer when running that program. Obviously, then, if it's up to a program to control your computer's input and output, every programming language must contain commands for input and output. In fact, a programming language without I/O commands would be about as useful to you as a book of matches would be to a fish. By providing commands for putting data into the computer and getting data back out again, a computer language allows you to create *interactive programs.*

BUZZWORD

Interactive Programs

Interactive programs allow two-way communication between the user and the computer. For example, the computer might output a question to the user by printing the question on-screen. The user can then answer the question by typing on his or her keyboard.

QBasic, like any other computer language, features several commands for controlling input and output. The PRINT command, for example, allows you to make text appear on the computer's screen. You might want to do this in order to ask the user a question, or you might print text on-screen to give the user a piece of information he or she requested. Suppose you want to print a simple message on-screen. Listing 3.1 is a short QBasic program that shows you how to do this. Load QBasic and type the program exactly as it is shown in Listing 3.1. The program is called

CHAPTER 3

HITHERE.BAS; after you type it, you should save it under that name. (You learned to save program files in Chapter 2, remember?)

Listing 3.1 HITHERE1.BAS prints text on-screen

Start every program by clearing the screen

```
CLS
PRINT "Hi, there!"
PRINT "What's a nice person like you"
PRINT "doing with a computer like this?"
```

Don't forget quotation marks

IN SIMPLE TERMS

Listing 3.1 is just about the simplest computer program you can write. First, the CLS command clears the computer's screen. Then the PRINT commands display three lines of text on your screen.

After you run Listing 3.1, you will see the following output:

```
Hi, there!
What's a nice person like you
doing with a computer like this?
```

As you can see, each PRINT command creates a single line of text on-screen. The text the command prints is the text that you place after the word PRINT. This text, called a *string literal*, must be enclosed in quotation marks.

BUZZWORD

String and String Literal

A string is a group of text characters. A string literal is text that you want the computer to use exactly as you type it. You tell the computer that a line of text is a string literal by enclosing the text in quotation marks.

Now, suppose you wanted the text printed on your printer instead of on-screen? In QBasic, this is easy to do. Just change all the PRINT commands in the program to LPRINT commands, as shown in Listing 3.2.

Listing 3.2 HITHERE2.BAS sends text to your printer

The **PRINT** command prints text on-screen

The **LPRINT** commands send text to your printer

```
CLS
PRINT "Printing..."
LPRINT "Hi, there!"
LPRINT "What's a nice person like you"
LPRINT "doing with a computer like this?"
```

IN SIMPLE TERMS

Listing 3.2 works much like Listing 3.1, except it sends text to your printer as well as on-screen. As before, the CLS command clears the screen. The PRINT command then prints a line of text on-screen. This line of text tells you that the computer is busy sending text to your printer. Finally, the LPRINT commands send three lines of text to your printer.

Notice in this program an extra line that displays the word Printing... on-screen. Without this line, the program's user would not know what the computer was doing until text started appearing on the printer. Your program should always tell the user what it's doing (if it's not immediately obvious), especially when it's doing any processing that takes more than a few seconds to complete. Nothing is quite as alarming to a computer user as watching a computer that seems to be doing nothing. You can spot alarmed computer users easily: They're the ones pounding their monitors, punching their computer's reset button, and screaming words we can't print in this book.

Here's what you see on-screen when you run Listing 3.2:

```
Printing...
```

QBASIC FOR ROOKIES

Now you know how to use QBasic to ask a computer user a question, which is one form of output. But how can you get the user's answer into your program? You could have the user write you a memo, but that's too slow. As you may have guessed, QBasic has a command, called INPUT, that can get both *numeric values* and *text* from the user. But before you can learn about the INPUT command, you need to understand variables.

BUZZWORD

Numeric Values vs. Text

Numeric values are values that can be used in mathematical operations. *Text*, on the other hand, consists of alphabetic characters, numeric characters (not values), and other symbols—such as punctuation—that you use to write words and sentences in English (or any other language for that matter). The stuff you're reading in this book is text.

Variables

(A comfy home for input)

You've already learned that when you input data into a computer, the computer stores that data in its memory. You can think of your computer's memory as millions of little boxes, each holding a single value. Normally, each little box is numbered, starting at zero. The actual number of boxes in your computer depends upon how much memory you have installed. Fig. 1 illustrates how memory looks.

Fig. 1

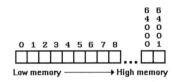

When you input data into your computer, a little guy named Benny grabs the data and runs away with it, giggling. Okay, I'm lying. Actually, your computer stuffs the data into one of those little boxes that make up its memory. (Benny's too busy sipping beer and watching exotic dancers at Al's Drink and Drool.) But in which box should the value be stored, and how can you refer to that box in a way that makes sense within a program? This is where variables come in.

Variables are really just memory boxes with names. Because you, the programmer, supply the names, you can name your variables almost anything you want, making your programs easier to read and understand. (You could even name a variable Benny, although why you'd want to is a mystery to most everyone on the planet.) When you first create a variable in your program, the memory box it represents contains a zero. Later in your program, you can store values in the memory box by referring to its name. For example, to keep track of the score in a game, you might have a variable named score. Whenever the player's score changes, you can put the new score value into the variable (memory box) named score. In this way, you've set aside a little piece of memory that contains data that your program requires.

You must, however, follow certain rules when you create variable names. First, a variable name must be no longer than 40 characters. Second, the name must start with a letter. The other characters can be letters, numbers, or a period. (You can't use spaces in a variable name. If necessary, however, you can use a period to separate words in the name.) Because QBasic isn't case sensitive, you can use any combination of upper- or lowercase letters in a variable name—the variable names Benny, benny, and BENNY all mean the same thing to QBasic. Finally, you can't use a QBasic keyword as a variable name.

Here are some *valid* variable names:

```
Total      Money.Spent      name23      AMOUNT
```

QBASIC FOR ROOKIES

Here are some *invalid* variable names:

```
3456      current_balance      Date Paid      PRINT
```

Variables and *INPUT*

(A tale of two buddies)

To get input into your programs, you need to use the INPUT command. INPUT commands and variables go together like Abbott and Costello: you must follow every INPUT command with the name of a variable. QBasic stores the input in the variable.

Suppose you're writing a program that needs to know the number of cars in a parking garage. Suppose also that when the user runs the program, the first thing he or she must do is input the current car count. This part of the program might look something like Listing 3.3.

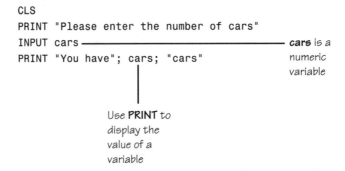

Listing 3.3 CARS1.BAS gets a value from the user

```
CLS
PRINT "Please enter the number of cars"
INPUT cars ────────────────────────────── cars is a
PRINT "You have"; cars; "cars"            numeric
                   │                       variable
                   │
          Use PRINT to
          display the
          value of a
          variable
```

**IN SIMPLE
TERMS**

Listing 3.3 clears the screen with the CLS command, and then prints a line of text on-screen that asks the user for the number of cars. Next, the INPUT command allows the user to type a number in response to the question. The number is stored in the variable cars. Finally, the program prints another line of text on-screen. This text is the string literal "You have", the value stored in the variable cars, and the string literal "cars".

Type Listing 3.3 into QBasic and run it. When you see a question mark on the screen, this is your cue to input a value into the program. Type any number you like, and press Enter. Your screen should resemble the following output. (We have used bold here to point out the number that a user would enter.)

```
Please enter the number of cars
? 3
You have 3 cars
```

Where did that question mark come from? The INPUT command puts the question mark on-screen to tell the user to input something into the program. In the program the word cars following the INPUT command is a variable name and is used to identify the little box in memory in which the response is stored.

Suppose you type the number 8 in response to the program. Fig. 2 illustrates what your computer's memory might look like. In this figure, QBasic has assigned the variable cars to memory location 6 and has placed the value 8 into that location. You don't have to worry about where QBasic puts variables in memory. QBasic handles all that for you.

Fig. 2

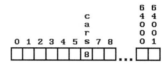

Now, back to the program shown in Listing 3.3. How about that last line? Pretty fancy-looking PRINT command, wouldn't you say? This example illustrates the power of the PRINT command. In this case, the PRINT command displays not only string literals, but also the value stored in the variable cars. See the semicolons? By using semicolons, you can build a line of text from different elements. In the PRINT command, the line of text that will be displayed on-screen includes three elements: the string literal "You have", the variable cars, and the string literal "cars". The semicolons tell the PRINT command to place each of these elements one after the other on the same line.

Notice that QBasic can easily tell the difference between the string literal "cars" and the variable cars. Now you know why the quotation marks are so important. In fact, without the quotation marks, QBasic would interpret each word following the PRINT command as a variable rather than as a string.

Numeric and String Variables

Variables can exist as many different types. You'll learn about variable types in the next chapter, but for now you can think of variables as holding either numeric values or text. For example, run Listing 3.3 again, and this time enter a word instead of a number. When you do, QBasic gives you the message Redo from start and prompts you to enter your response again. You receive this message because you can't store text in a variable that's supposed to hold a numeric value. Here's what your output would look like this time:

```
Please enter the number of cars
? three

Redo from start
? 3
You have 3 cars
```

CAUTION

You can never store text input in a numeric variable. Consequently, when a user types text in response to an INPUT statement that's expecting a numeric value, QBasic prints the strange error message Redo from start. This poorly written message is really trying to say "Please reenter your input." In other words, QBasic is giving you another chance to input a valid value.

You can, however, create a variable for holding text—a string variable. In fact, you did this in Chapter 2 when you ran the program that prints your name on the screen. To create a string variable, just add a dollar sign ($) to the variable's name, as shown in Listing 3.4.

Listing 3.4 CARS2.BAS gets text from the user

cars is now a string variable ──────

```
CLS
PRINT "Please enter the number of cars"
INPUT cars$
PRINT "You have "; cars$; " cars"
```

When you run the program in Listing 3.4, you are asked to enter the number of cars. In this case, however, whatever you type is treated as text, not as a numeric value, which means you can type *Three* or 3. Note that numbers entered as text cannot be used as numeric values; that is, they cannot be used in mathematical calculations.

IN SIMPLE TERMS

As in previous programs, Listing 3.4 first clears the screen with the CLS command. It then prints a line of text to the screen, asking the user for the number of cars. Next, the INPUT command asks the user to use the keyboard to type a text string in response to the question. The text the user types is stored in the string variable cars$. Finally, the program prints another line of text to the screen. This text is a combination of string literals and the value stored in cars$.

Here's the output from Listing 3.4:

```
Please enter the number of cars
? three
You have three cars
```

PLAY BALL!

BUZZWORD

Numeric and String Variables

A numeric variable can hold only numeric values. A string variable can hold only text.

Look at the last line of this program. Do you see something different? The first string literal, "You have ", ends with a space, and the second string literal, " cars", starts with a space. If you remove these spaces, the text string printed on your screen looks something like the following:

```
You havethreecars.
```

Why didn't you have this problem with the first version of this program (CARS1.BAS)? Because that version used a numeric variable. When QBasic prints a numeric variable, it always leaves space for a minus sign

in front of the value. If the value is positive, all you see is the extra space because QBasic doesn't print the positive sign. However, if the value is negative, you'll see the negative sign. Run CARS1.BAS again, and this time enter a negative number, such as –3. You'll see the following output:

```
Please enter the number of cars
? -3
You have -3 cars
```

You can't have a negative number of cars in your garage (at least, not in this universe), so you don't have to worry about the negative sign in this program.

In addition to the space for a minus sign, QBasic always places a space after a numeric variable. However, string variables are never printed with extra spaces, so to make the output look right you have to add spaces wherever necessary (unless, of course, you want the strings to run together).

Combining *PRINT* and *INPUT*

(It's two commands in one!)

An INPUT command without a prompt is as confusing as a David Lynch film. After all, unless you tell the user what you expect him to enter, how will he know what to do? (This, of course, doesn't apply to programs written for mind readers.) Because you frequently need to prompt for information in programs, QBasic provides a special form of the INPUT command that lets you display a prompt without using PRINT. Listing 3.5 is a new version of the CARS program that uses this technique.

QBASIC FOR ROOKIES

You can make
a prompt
part of
the **INPUT** ————
command

Listing 3.5 CARS3.BAS's *INPUT* command includes the prompt

```
CLS
INPUT "Please enter the number of cars"; cars$
PRINT "You have "; cars$; " cars"
```

**IN SIMPLE
TERMS**

Listing 3.5 first clears the screen with the CLS command. Then the INPUT command prints a prompt to the screen and enables the user to type a text string in response to the prompt. The text the user types is stored in the string variable cars$. Finally, the program prints another line of text to the screen. This text is a combination of string literals and the value stored in cars$.

In Listing 3.5, the prompt is placed immediately after the INPUT command. Then, a semicolon separates the text prompt from the input variable, cars$. The following shows the output for Listing 3.5:

```
Please enter the number of cars? three
You have three cars
```

Notice that the question mark no longer appears on its own line; it now follows the prompt. Because of this change, it might be better to reword the prompt to say something like How many cars, so the question mark will make more sense.

Fun With *INPUT* and *PRINT*

(Almost coffee break time)

Now that you've learned a little about QBasic input and output, how about finishing up with a program that puts all you've learned to the test? Type Listing 3.6 into the QBasic editor. When you run the program, it beeps and asks you to enter your first name. After you enter your first name, the program beeps again and asks for your last name. Finally, after you enter your last name, the program changes the screen colors and prints a colorful message.

Listing 3.6 CLRBEEP.BAS beeps and changes the text color

Beep gets
user's
attention

Printing text
in color makes
screens more
attractive

```
CLS
BEEP
INPUT "What's your first name"; firstname$
BEEP
INPUT "What's your last name"; lastname$
COLOR 14, 1
PRINT
PRINT "Hello there, "; firstname$; " "; lastname$; "!"
```

Here's the output for Listing 3.6. Remember, you must have a color monitor to be able to see the different colors.

```
What's your first name? Uncle
What's your last name? Henry

Hello there, Uncle Henry!
```

**IN SIMPLE
TERMS**

Listing 3.6 first clears the screen with the CLS command. Then the BEEP command beeps your computer's speaker. The first INPUT command prints a prompt and allows you to enter

continues

continued

your first name, which is stored in the string variable `firstname$`. After another beep, the next `INPUT` command allows you to enter your last name, which is stored in the string variable `lastname$`. Finally, the `COLOR` command changes the screen colors, and the two `PRINT` commands print a blank line and the final message.

In Listing 3.6, you learn two new commands. The `BEEP` command makes your computer's speaker beep. The `COLOR` command lets you set the text colors. This command requires one or more *arguments*, separated by commas, that tell QBasic which colors you want. The first number is the text color (foreground color), the second number is the text background color, and the third number (used only for CGA graphics) is the screen border color.

BUZZWORD

Argument

An *argument* is a value that is required by a command. For example, the text you place after a `PRINT` command is that command's argument. Similarly, the color values you type after the `COLOR` command are that command's arguments.

What third number? In Listing 3.6, there are only two numbers because the program sets only the text and text background colors. In other words, you don't need to include all three numbers. You only need to include numbers for the colors you want to change. To change just the text color, use the command `COLOR N`, where `N` is the number of the color you want. If you don't want to change the text color, but do want to change the text background color, use the command `COLOR , N`. By including a comma for the first argument, QBasic knows that `N` is for the

text background. The color values you can use are shown in the following table.

Color Value	Color Displayed
0	Black
1	Blue
2	Green
3	Cyan
4	Red
5	Magenta
6	Brown
7	White
8	Gray
9	Light Blue
10	Light Green
11	Light Cyan
12	Light Red
13	Light Magenta
14	Yellow
15	Bright White

Note: *Color values 8 through 15 affect the foreground color only.*

CAUTION

When using the COLOR command, make sure you don't set the text color to the same value as the background color. If you do, any text you print will be invisible. Most people have a heck of a time reading invisible text!

Common Rookie Mistakes

Missing or incorrect punctuation: Novice programmers tend to overlook the importance of punctuation characters such as semicolons and commas in commands. Every character in a program is important. Be careful not to overlook any.

Misspelled variable names: Incorrectly spelling a variable name creates program bugs that are difficult to find. For example, suppose you have in your program a variable named Total.Numbers. As you type the lines of your program, you accidentally spell this variable as TotalNumbers. To QBasic, Total.Numbers and TotalNumbers are different variables, each with their own value.

Sloppy formatting of text output: Make sure your program's text output contains spaces where needed and that all text is spelled correctly. Sloppy output is the mark of an amateur.

Summing Up

▼ Input and output devices transfer data to and from a computer.

▼ Most I/O is controlled by the currently running program.

▼ The PRINT command prints a line of text on-screen. This command's arguments may be string literals or variables. If you supply no arguments, PRINT prints a blank line.

▼ String literals must be enclosed in quotation marks.

▼ The LPRINT command works much like the PRINT command, except it sends its output to a printer.

▼ Your computer's memory can be thought of as a series of little boxes. Each box can hold a single value.

▼ Variables are named places in memory where you can store data.

▼ Numeric variables can hold only numeric values. String variables can hold only text (or numbers that the computer treats as text).

▼ The INPUT command requests input from a user. The input is stored in the variable indicated by the command.

▼ By adding a prompt to the INPUT command, you don't need a separate PRINT command to display the prompt.

▼ The BEEP command makes your computer's speaker beep.

▼ The COLOR command lets you change text colors.

Now that you understand basic I/O, you're ready to take a closer look at the way variables work. In Chapter 4, you learn about many different types of variables and how to use them in mathematical operations.

CHAPTER 4
Crunching Numbers
(The Dreaded Math Chapter)

IN A NUTSHELL

▼ Using variables in mathematical expressions
▼ Understanding arithmetic operations
▼ Handling the order of operations
▼ Using different data types

QBASIC FOR ROOKIES

You've probably heard that programming a computer requires lots of math. And if you're like most people, all those formulas and equations you learned in high school now look stranger than an ostrich at a square dance. Guess what? Most programs require only simple mathematical calculations—addition, subtraction, multiplication, and division—the same stuff you do every day.

Moreover, when you're writing a program, you won't have to wear down pencils adding long columns of numbers or fry your brain trying to figure out 35,764 divided by 137. The computer can do the calculations for you. If you know how to use the basic arithmetic operations to solve simple problems, you know all the math necessary to write a computer program. Computer programming is more logical than mathematical. It's just a matter of common sense. (If you have trouble remembering to come in out of the rain, computer programming may not be for you.)

Still, you can't avoid math entirely. Heaven knows, your humble author has tried. Computers, after all, are number-crunching machines that like nothing better than spitting out the results of hundreds, thousands, or even millions of calculations. It's up to you, the wise programmer, to give the computer the commands it needs to perform these calculations. In this chapter, you'll learn to do just that.

Variables and Math

(The astounding, uncensored story)

In Chapter 3, you learned about variables—the little boxes in memory in which your program stores numbers. Unlike a constant, such as the number 3, variables can represent almost any value—except maybe the balance on my Visa card (a number so large even a computer has a tough time remembering it). Variables are extremely valuable entities. Because variables represent numbers, you can use them in mathematical operations.

PLAY BALL!

BUZZWORD

> **Constant**
>
> A *constant* is a value that cannot be changed in your program. Numbers that you type directly into your program are constants. String literals also are constants.

For example, suppose you run a small video store, and you want to know how many tapes you have. You might think to yourself, "I've got 20 copies of *Naughty Banshees from Venus*, 50 copies of *Dances with Muskrats*, and 10 copies of *Ren and Stimpy's 60-Minute Workout*. So, I've got 80 videotapes." If you want to use the computer to solve this mathematical problem, you would load QBasic and type **PRINT 20+50+10** into the immediate-command window. The computer would print the answer: 80. Just as it did when you were in school, the + symbol means addition to a computer program.

There's a better way, however, to solve the videotape problem—one that works with any number of videotapes. This new method uses variables in mathematical operations. As you've learned, you can call a variable just about anything you like. (Yes, you can even call a variable `late.for.dinner`.) Names such as `naughty`, `dances`, and `stimpy` are completely acceptable. Beginning to see the light? Look over the TAPES1.BAS program in Listing 4.1.

Listing 4.1 TAPES1.BAS adds three variables

```
CLS
PRINT "Enter number of Naughty Banshees"
INPUT naughty
PRINT "Enter number of Dances With Muskrats"
INPUT dances
PRINT "Enter number of Ren & Stimpy's"
INPUT stimpy
tapes = naughty + dances + stimpy
PRINT "Total number of tapes: ";
PRINT tapes
```

Tape counts are entered by user → (points to INPUT naughty)

Three variables are added; result is placed in another variable → (points to tapes = naughty + dances + stimpy)

73

CHAPTER 4

**IN SIMPLE
TERMS**

Listing 4.1 clears the screen, and then asks how many of each of the three tapes you have in inventory. Your answers are stored in the variables naughty, dances, and stimpy. The program then adds these three variables and places the total in the variable tapes. Finally, the program prints the total number of tapes.

This program asks you how many copies you have of each videotape. As you type your answers, the computer zaps those answers into the variables naughty, dances, and stimpy. Then, the program adds the variables and plunks the total into another variable called tapes. Finally, the program displays the number contained in tapes. Now you know the following two things:

1. You have 80 videotapes in your store.

2. With movie titles like these, you'll be out of business faster than your customer can say, "Dances with WHAT?"

Here's the output from Listing 4.1:

```
Enter number of Naughty Banshees
? 20
Enter number of Dances with Muskrats
? 50
Enter number of Ren & Stimpy's
? 10
Total number of tapes:  80
```

By using a program similar to this one, you can get a new tape total any-time you like. Just provide your program with new counts for each movie.

Guess what? You just used math in a computer program. It didn't hurt a bit, did it?

Beyond Addition

(More of the uncensored story)

Of course, computers can do more than add. They can perform any basic arithmetic operation. QBasic even has functions for figuring out things like square roots and absolute values. If you don't know what a square root or an absolute value is, don't hit the panic button; you still won't have trouble programming your computer. Just don't plan to write an algebra tutorial anytime soon.

Let's assume that your videotape store is still thriving, despite its horrible selection and the fact that the local chapter of Citizens Against Pain-fully Stupid Movies has a contract out on your head. Suppose you now want to find the total value of your inventory, as well as the average cost per tape. To find the total value of your inventory, multiply each title's price by the number of copies you own. Perform this calculation for all titles, and then add those amounts together to get the total value. To find the average value per tape, divide the total value by the total num-ber of tapes. You could calculate these totals using a program similar to Listing 4.2.

Listing 4.2 TAPES2.BAS figures the total and average values

```
CLS
PRINT "How much is Banshees?"
INPUT price
PRINT "How many Banshees do you have?"
INPUT quantity
total.num.tapes = quantity
total.value = price * quantity
PRINT "How much is Dances?"
INPUT price
PRINT "How many Dances do you have?"
INPUT quantity
total.num.tapes = total.num.tapes + quantity
total.value = total.value + price * quantity
PRINT "How much is Ren & Stimpy's?"
INPUT price
PRINT "How many Ren & Stimpy's do you have?"
INPUT quantity
total.num.tapes = total.num.tapes + quantity
total.value = total.value + price * quantity
average.value = total.value / total.num.tapes
PRINT
PRINT "The total value of all tapes is:"
PRINT "$"; total.value
PRINT "The average value is:"
PRINT "$"; average.value
```

The variable **total.num.tapes** begins at the same value as number of Banshees

Multiplication is used to calculate the price of all tapes

The right side is done before the left

Don't forget order of operations!

IN SIMPLE TERMS

The program in Listing 4.2 begins by clearing the screen and asking for the price and quantity of the first video title. These values are temporarily stored in the variables price and quantity. The quantity is then placed in the variable total.num.tapes. The total value for all tapes with that title is calculated by multiplying the price of the tape by the quantity; that total is stored in the variable total.value.

Next, the program asks for the price and quantity of the second title. After the program receives that information, it adds the quantity for the second title to `total.num.tapes` (which contains the quantity for the first title). This total is the combined quantity for the first two titles. The total value for the two titles is calculated by multiplying the second tape's price by its quantity and adding that amount to `total.value`.

Notice how the program reuses the variables `price` and `quantity`. You don't have to save the price and quantity of each tape after you've added them to the running totals; therefore, you can use `price` and `quantity` as input variables for every `INPUT` statement. Every time you use `price` and `quantity` in an `INPUT` statement, the new value the user enters is stored there.

The third tape is processed the same way as the first two. The average value for all tapes is then calculated by dividing `total.value` by `total.num.tapes`. Finally, after printing a blank line, the program prints the total value for all three tapes, along with the average value per tape.

Here is the output from Listing 4.2. The numbers that appear in bold represent the values you would provide.

```
How much is Banshees?
? 29.95
How many Banshees do you have?
? 12
How much is Dances?
? 34.95
```

```
How many Dances do you have?
? 23
How much is Ren & Stimpy's?
? 14.98
How many Ren & Stimpy's do you have?
? 8


The total value of all tapes is:
$ 1283.09
The average value is:
$ 29.8393
```

This program is a bit longer than the first one, but it still uses only basic arithmetic. It's longer because it performs more calculations than the first example.

What's going on here? This program first asks you for the price and quantity of each tape you have in stock. The program then calculates the total value of all the tapes in your store, as well as your average value per tape. If you look at the program carefully, you'll see something strange about `total.num.tapes`. Specifically, what the heck does the line `total.num.tapes = total.num.tapes + quantity` do? How can the same variable be on both sides of an equation? Why do I keep asking these dumb questions?

First, you have to stop thinking that the equal sign (=) always means *equals*. It doesn't. In QBasic arithmetic operations, this symbol actually means *takes the value of*, which makes it an *assignment operator*. (Even in programming, however, the equal sign still can mean *is equal to*, as you'll learn in Chapter 6, "Making Decisions.")

You also must understand that QBasic interprets statements from right to left. Therefore, in Listing 4.2 `total.num.tapes` and `quantity` are added first, and then the result of the addition is assigned back to `total.num.tapes`—that is, the result is stored in `total.num.tapes`—wiping out the value that was there previously.

QBASIC FOR ROOKIES

PLAY BALL!

BUZZWORD

Assignment Operator

An *assignment operator* is used to assign a value to a variable. In QBasic, the assignment operator is an equal sign, but other computer languages may use different assignment operators. In Pascal, for example, the assignment operator is a colon followed by an equal sign (`:=`).

Confused? How about an example? Suppose `total.num.tapes` is equal to 7 and `quantity` is equal to 3. When the computer sees the line `total.num.tapes = total.num.tapes + quantity`, it adds 7 to 3 and pops the value 10 into `total.num.tapes`. Using this method, you can add values to a variable that already holds a value. You'll do this often in your programs.

As you can see, a QBasic program uses an asterisk (`*`) to represent multiplication, not an `x` as you might expect. Division is represented by the forward slash character (`/`) because the computer keyboard doesn't have a division symbol. You could try painting a division symbol on one of your keys, but you'll still have to use the slash character in your programs.

The following table displays all of the QBasic arithmetic operators.

Operator	Name	Use
+	Addition	Sum values
−	Subtraction	Subtract values
*	Multiplication	Multiply values

continues

79

continued

Operator	Name	Use
/	Division	Divide values
\	Integer division	Determine the whole number result of division
^	Exponentiation	Raise a value to a power
MOD	Modulus	Determine the remainder of division

This next table shows some examples of mathematical operations using the arithmetic operators.

Operation	Result
5+8	13
12–7	5
3*6	18
10/3	3.333333
10\3	3
2^3	8
10 MOD 3	1

TIP

When you use regular division, denoted by the forward slash character (/), you are performing the type of division you learned in school. You may end up with a result like 2 (such as in the operation 4/2) or a result like 2.4 (such as in the operation 12/5).

When you use integer division, denoted by the backslash character (\), your answer will always be an integer because QBasic drops any part of the result that lies to the right of the decimal point. With integer division, then, the operation 12\5 results in 2, rather than 2.4.

The MOD operator performs division, too, but it only gives you the remainder of the division. For example, 4 goes into 14 3 times with a remainder of 2, so the operation 14 MOD 4 yields a result of 2. As a beginning programmer, you probably won't have much use for this operator.

Finally, the exponentiation operator (^) is used to raise numbers to a power. When you raise a number to a power, you multiply the number times itself the number of times indicated by the exponent (the number after the ^ character). For example, 10^2 is the same as 10 * 10, which equals 100. The operation 5^3 is the same as 5 * 5 * 5, which equals 125.

Order of Operations

(Me first! Me first!)

Another curious line in Listing 4.2 is `total.value = total.value + price * quantity`. This program line is similar to the line that calculates the total number of tapes, but it contains both an addition and multiplication operation. This brings up the important topic of operator precedence or, as it's more commonly known, the order of operations.

If you were to add `total.value` to `price` and then multiply the sum by `quantity`, you'd get an incorrect result. Operator precedence dictates that all multiplication must take place before any addition. So in the preceding line, `total.value` is calculated by first multiplying `price` times `quantity` and then adding that product to `total.value`.

Don't forget about operator precedence; if you do, your calculations won't be accurate and your programs won't run correctly. Not adhering to the rules of operator precedence can also affect your home life: broken programs make for grumpy programmers, and grumpy programmers are no fun to have around.

The order of operations for QBasic is exponentiation first; then multiplication, division, integer division, and MOD; and finally, addition and subtraction. Operations of the same precedence are evaluated from left to right. For example, in the expression

```
3 * 5 / 2
```

3 is first multiplied by 5, which gives a result of 15. This result is then divided by 2, giving a result of 7.5. The QBasic operator precedence is summarized in the following table.

Order	Operator	Name
1	∧	Exponentiation
2	* / \ MOD	Multiplication, division, integer division, and modulus
3	+ −	Addition and subtraction

You can change operator precedence by using parentheses. For example, suppose you wanted the addition in the line `total.value = total.value + price * quantity` to be calculated before the multiplication. You could rewrite the line as `total.value = (total.value + price) * quantity`. Any operation enclosed in parentheses is performed first. Consequently, `total.value` and `price` are added first, and the sum is then multiplied by `quantity`.

TIP

When you write a program line that contains many arithmetic operations, you might want to use parentheses to more clearly indicate the order of operation. For example, the formula

```
total.value = total.value + (price * quantity)
```

is easier to read than the original formula

```
total.value = total.value + price * quantity
```

Both formulas, however, yield the same result.

Data Types

(What's a nice integer like you doing in a program like this?)

You'll be happy to know you're almost finished with the math stuff. You only have to explore one more topic before you move on: data types. You've already had a little experience with data types, but you probably didn't realize it at the time.

When you used numeric variables and string variables, you were using variables of two different data types. Numeric variables can hold only numbers, and string variables can hold only text strings. What you haven't learned is that numeric variables can be divided into many other data types, including integers, long integers, single-precision, and double-precision.

NOTE

> Although numeric variables can hold only numbers and string variables can hold only text strings, that doesn't mean a string variable can't hold a character that represents a number. For example, when assigned to a numeric variable, the number 3 represents a value that can be used in arithmetic operations. However, the character 3 assigned to a string variable is just a text character—no different from any other text character, such as A or Z. Although a string variable can hold number characters, those characters cannot be used directly in mathematical operations.

Until now, you've been concerned only with giving your numeric variables appropriate names; you haven't worried about what type of value they would hold. You could ignore a variable's data type because QBasic can determine data types on its own. But what if you want to be sure

that a variable always contains a certain type of data, no matter what type of assignment operation it's involved in? For example, what if you want to add two real numbers, but you want to store the result as an integer? What are real numbers and integers, anyway?

An *integer* is any whole number, such as 23, 76, –65, or 1200. Notice that none of these numbers contain a decimal portion, and none of them are smaller than –32,768 or greater than 32,767. A QBasic integer must fall into this range.

What if you need to use a number that doesn't fit into the integer range? You can use a long integer. A *long integer* resembles an integer in that it can hold only a whole number. However, the range of a long integer is much larger: –2,147,483,648 to 2,147,483,647, to be exact. Unless you're trying to calculate the national debt or count the number of times Elizabeth Taylor has been married, you're not likely to need values larger than these.

Numbers that contain a decimal portion are called *floating-point* or *real* numbers. Like integers, they come in two flavors. A *single-precision real number* is accurate out to six decimal places (for example, 34.875637). A *double-precision real number*, on the other hand, is accurate out to 14 decimal places (for example, 657.36497122357638). Real numbers in QBasic can be very tiny or incredibly large.

CAUTION

When writing a program, you may be tempted to make all your integer variables long integers and all your real-number variables double-precision. When you do this, you no longer have to worry about whether your values go out of range. However, this technique has two drawbacks. First, long integers and double-precision real numbers take up more memory than their smaller counterparts. Second, your

continues

QBASIC FOR ROOKIES

continued

computer takes longer to access and manipulate these larger values, so using them can significantly slow down your programs. Use long integers and double-precision values only when you really need them.

Remember in Chapter 2 when you learned about string variables? You learned that to create a variable of this data type you had to add a dollar sign to the variable's name. The various numeric data types also have suffixes that tell QBasic the type of data the variable holds. To specify a particular data type, you only have to add the appropriate suffix to the variable's name. The following table shows the various data types and their corresponding suffixes.

Type	Suffix	Example
Integer	%	`total%`
Long integer	&	`count&`
Single precision	!	`value!`
Double precision	#	`weight#`
String	$	`name$`

NOTE

Like a variable, a constant has a data type. The difference is that the data type is implicit. For example, 10 is an integer, 23.7564 is a single-precision real number, and "Alexander" is a string. You can tell what the data type is just by looking at the value, and so can QBasic.

Listing 4.3 is a revised version of Listing 4.2 that uses specific data types for its variables. This program works the same as the original; the only difference is that each variable name now includes a suffix that tells QBasic the type of data that can be stored in the variable. By looking over the listing, you can see which variables hold integers and which hold single-precision values. (*Hint:* Look for the % and ! suffixes.)

Listing 4.3 TAPES3.BAS uses specific data types

```
CLS
PRINT "How much is Banshees?"
INPUT price!                                          Single-precision
PRINT "How many Banshees do you have?"                variable
INPUT quantity%
total.num.tapes% = quantity%        Integer variables
total.value! = price! * quantity%
PRINT "How much is Dances?"
INPUT price!
PRINT "How many Dances do you have?"
INPUT quantity%
total.num.tapes% = total.num.tapes% + quantity%
total.value! = total.value! + price! * quantity%
PRINT "How much is Ren & Stimpy's?"
INPUT price!
PRINT "How many Ren & Stimpy's do you have?"
INPUT quantity%
total.num.tapes% = total.num.tapes% + quantity%
total.value! = total.value! + price! * quantity%
average.value! = total.value! / total.num.tapes%
PRINT
PRINT "The total value of all tapes is:"
PRINT "$"; total.value!
PRINT "The average value is:"
PRINT "$"; average.value!
```

Integer variables ————

Variable on left of assignment operator ———— is single-precision real number; result of calculation will be single-precision real number

Listing 4.3 is virtually identical to Listing 4.2. The difference is that now every variable in the program has a specific data type, which is denoted by the variable's suffix. When you look at the program line `INPUT price!`, you know that the variable `price!` is a single-precision real number. The exclamation point added to the variable's name tells you this. Likewise, in the line `INPUT quantity%`, you know that the variable `quantity%` is an integer, because it has a percent sign as a suffix.

But what about a line like `total.value! = price! * quantity%`? Here, you're multiplying a real number, `price!`, times an integer, `quantity%`. Seems like the old case of apples and oranges, doesn't it? In a way, it is. You must be careful when mixing data types in expressions, to be sure you get the result you expect. The data type you'll end up with is the one on the left of the equal sign. In this case, the variable on the left of the equal sign, `total.value!`, is a single-precision real number; therefore, the result of the multiplication will be a single-precision real number.

A final note: Unless the expression contains only integers, be especially careful when you assign the results of a calculation to an integer. You could receive an incorrect result. For example, the line `result% = 13.5 * 3.3` makes `result%` equal to 45, not 44.55 as you might expect. Why? The variable `result%` is an integer, so it cannot hold a real number like 44.55. When QBasic solves this expression, it first multiplies 13.5 times 3.3 to get the result of 44.55. QBasic then rounds this answer to the nearest integer, which is 45, because you've asked it to store the answer as an integer. QBasic assumes that you know what you're doing and gives you no warning of the conversion.

Common Rookie Mistakes

Misinterpreting the equal sign. When used in arithmetic operations in QBasic, the equal sign means *takes the value of*. It is an assignment operator.

Using the wrong symbol for an arithmetic operator. The symbol for multiplication in QBasic is the asterisk (*), not an x. Also, be sure you know the difference between a slash (/), which is the division operator, and a backslash (\), which is the integer division operator.

Overlooking operator precedence. If you want to be sure your formulas yield correct results, double-check the formula's order of operations. Better still, use parentheses in your formulas to ensure that all arithmetic operations are done in the order you expect.

Using the wrong data type. Remember that integers cannot hold values outside the range –32,768 to 32,767. If you try to assign a value outside this range to an integer variable, you'll get an overflow error. The other data types also have limited ranges. However, their ranges are so much larger than the integer's, you're not likely to run into values too small or too large for them.

Incorrectly mixing data types. You will often need to use different data types in arithmetic operations. When you write these types of expressions, remember that QBasic assumes that you know what you're doing and will automatically make whatever conversions are required. Be especially careful when you assign the results of a real-number calculation to an integer. In this case, QBasic always rounds the result to the nearest integer.

Summing Up

▼ Computer programming requires more logic than math. However, you can't avoid some mathematical operations in your programs.

▼ Variables can hold any value you assign to them, whereas constants never change. Because variables can change value in your programs, you can use them to represent numbers whose values you don't know ahead of time.

▼ You can perform all normal arithmetic operations with QBasic, including addition (+), subtraction (-), multiplication (*), and division (/). Other operations available are integer division (\), exponentiation (^), and modulus (MOD).

▼ When used in arithmetic expressions, the equal sign (=) acts as an assignment operator.

▼ All arithmetic expressions in QBasic follow the standard rules of operator precedence (order of operations).

▼ Variables and constants in a QBasic program can be one of many data types, including integer, long integer, single-precision real, double-precision real, and string.

In this chapter, you've learned a lot about using math and data types in QBasic. You'll run into these topics again in this book, but you'll be glad to know that the worst is behind you. (Hooray!) In the next chapter, you'll take a closer look at the string data type, which allows you to manipulate text in your programs in many ways.

CHAPTER 5
Working with Text
(A Frank Textual Discussion)

IN A NUTSHELL

▼ Joining strings
▼ Using string lengths
▼ Handling substrings
▼ Converting strings and numbers

Pictures of bathing beauties (or well-oiled hunks) may be more fun to look at than a screen full of words and numbers; the simple truth, however, is that most information displayed on your computer screen is in text form. This fact separates computer users into two groups: those who would rather hang out at the beach, and those who understand that computers were designed to help humans deal with large amounts of information—information most often presented as text.

Because text displays are so important in computing, QBasic has a number of functions and commands that manipulate text. These *functions* enable you to join two or more strings into one, find the length of a string, extract a small portion of a string, or convert numbers to strings or strings to numbers. In this chapter, you'll learn to use many of QBasic's string-handling functions. If, however, you're still more interested in bathing beauties, shut down your computer and go back to gazing longingly at the *Sports Illustrated* swimsuit issue. The rest of you, follow me.

Joining Strings

(Till death do they part)

You'll often have two or more strings in your programs that you must combine into one. For example, you may have a user's first name and last name in two separate strings. In order to get the user's entire name into a single string, you have to *concatenate* (join together end-to-end) the two strings. Use QBasic's concatenation operator, which looks like an addition operator, to handle this string-handling task. To join three strings, for example, type the following:

```
string1$ + string2$ + string3$
```

QBASIC FOR ROOKIES

PLAY BALL!

BUZZWORD

Concatenation

Concatenation is the process of joining two or more strings end-to-end to create one large string. QBasic performs concatenation with the plus sign (+), which acts as the string-concatenation operator.

Simply joining the strings, however, is not a complete program statement; you also must tell QBasic where to store the new string. To do this, use QBasic's assignment operator, the equal sign (=). The assignment operator for strings works just like the assignment operator for numeric variables. For example, to make the string variable `insult$` equal to the text string `Your breath is strong enough to lift a horse`, use the command

```
insult$ = "Your breath is strong enough to lift a horse"
```

To see how all this works, look at Listing 5.1.

Listing 5.1 NAME1.BAS joins two strings

Note space
added
between the
two strings

```
CLS
INPUT "Enter your first name: ", first$
INPUT "Enter your last name: ", last$
name$ = first$ + " " + last$
PRINT
PRINT "Your full name is: "; name$
```

IN SIMPLE
TERMS

Listing 5.1 clears the screen and then asks you to enter your first and last names. The names are stored in the variables `first$` and `last$`, respectively. The program then joins the two strings (with a space character between them) using the

continues

93

QBASIC FOR ROOKIES

continued

concatenation operator, and the result is stored in the string variable name$. Finally, after printing a blank line, the program prints your full name on the screen.

CATCH THIS!

Do you see something different about the INPUT commands in Listing 5.1? Look at the INPUT command in the second line. See the comma separating the prompt from the input variable first$? The comma here, instead of the usual semicolon, tells QBasic not to print the question mark that usually appears when you use an INPUT command. This technique enables you to create any type of prompt you need. Pretty tricky, eh?

When you run the NAME1.BAS program in Listing 5.1, you are asked to type your first name and then your last name. The program then prints your full name on-screen. It's not the fact that your name is displayed that makes this program interesting—you already know how to use a PRINT statement to display output. What's interesting is that the final output is in a single string, name$, not in the two original name strings, first$ and last$. This single string is created by using QBasic's string assignment operator (=) and string concatenation operator (+) to join the two original name strings.

Listing 5.1 delivers the following output:

```
Enter your first name: Freddy
Enter your last name: Kruger
Your full name is: Freddy Kruger
```

The Length of a String

(The long and short of it)

Every string has a length: the number of characters contained in that string. For example, the string Why did the chicken cross the road? has a length of 35, because it contains 35 characters. (Spaces are characters, too.) The string Because the farmer was chasing him with a hatchet! has a length of 50. Theoretically, a string can have any length, from 0 to infinity. In QBasic, however, a string is much more conservative and can be any length from 0 to 32,767 characters.

PLAY BALL!

BUZZWORD

Null String

A *null string* is a string that contains 0 characters. How can a string contain 0 characters? Easy! When you assign a string variable to an empty string, you get a string with a length of 0, as shown in the following example:

```
string1$ = ""
```

Notice that there are no characters between the quotation marks. This creates an empty, or null, string. At first, you may think creating a null string makes about as much sense as drinking from an empty glass. But sometimes you may want to initialize a string variable to a null string so that you'll know the string doesn't contain old data.

Sometimes in your program, you may need to know the length of a string. For example, you might want to calculate the position of a string on-screen in which the position of one string depends on where a

previous string ends. To find the length of a string variable, use QBasic's LEN function, as in the following:

```
length% = LEN(string1$)
```

Here, the function's single argument, string1$, is the string for which you want the length. The LEN function returns the length of the string as a numeric value that can be used anywhere you can use a numeric value.

NOTE

Notice that the previous paragraph refers to a string variable called string1$. Why is there a number after the name? The number is actually part of the variable's name and is required because string$ is the name of a QBasic function. *Remember:* You can't use QBasic function names or keywords as variable names, so you must change (or add) at least one character to set the variable name apart from the keyword or function name. Please refer to Chapter 3 if you need to review the rules for creating variable names.

What the heck is a function, anyway? A function is simply a command that performs a specific task and then sends a result (returns a value) back to your program. The result returned from a function is called a *return value*. In the preceding paragraph, for example, you learned that LEN is a function that calculates the number of characters in a string. After doing this calculation, LEN sends the number of characters back to you, so that you can use it in your program. Usually, you assign a function's return value to a variable.

QBasic features two types of functions. The first type includes QBasic's built-in functions such as LEN, ABS (absolute value), and SQR (square root). QBasic boasts dozens of built-in functions that you can use in your programs. QBasic also lets you write your own functions, which usually

include several program lines that perform a specific task. You'll learn about this second type of function in Chapter 9.

PLAY BALL!

BUZZWORD

Function Call

A *function call* in QBasic consists of a function name followed by parentheses that contain the function's arguments. A function call always returns a single value (sends a value back to your program), which you usually store in a variable. In the case of the LEN function, the return value is the number of characters in the string used as the argument. In other words, when you use the LEN function, it sends the string's character count back to your program.

Listing 5.2 is a revised version of Listing 5.1 that uses the LEN function. If you've already typed Listing 5.1, simply add the last two lines of Listing 5.2 to the end of Listing 5.1. Then use the Save **A**s... command from QBasic's **F**ile menu to save the new program under its own name.

Listing 5.2 NAME2.BAS joins two strings and displays their lengths

LEN *returns the number of characters in a string*

```
CLS
INPUT "Enter your first name: ", first$
INPUT "Enter your last name: ", last$
name$ = first$ + " " + last$
PRINT
PRINT "Your full name is "; name$
length% = LEN(name$)
PRINT "The length of your name is"; length%
```

IN SIMPLE TERMS

Listing 5.2 is identical to Listing 5.1 except for the last two lines. The first new line gets the length of the string variable `name$` and saves it in the integer variable `length%`. The second new line displays the value of `length%`.

The following is the output from Listing 5.2:

```
Enter your first name: James
Enter your last name: Bond

Your full name is James Bond
The length of your name is 10
```

TIP

In Listing 5.2, you don't have to use the variable `length%`. You could rewrite the last two lines as one, like this:

```
PRINT "The length of your name is"; LEN(name$)
```

This method demonstrates how you can use functions in the same way you use numbers or numeric variables.

Extracting a Substring

(Bits and pieces)

Just as you can concatenate strings to create a larger string, you can separate strings into smaller strings called *substrings*. You might think that because you use the plus sign to perform concatenation, you would use the minus sign to extract substrings. If you try this, however, you'll annoy QBasic and embarrass yourself in front of your friends. The truth is, the minus sign serves no purpose when working with strings. Instead,

QBasic has several special string-handling functions that were created especially to extract whatever portion of a string you need. These string-handling functions are LEFT$, RIGHT$, and MID$.

PLAY BALL!

BUZZWORD

Substring
A *substring* is a portion of a larger string. For example, the string Twitdum is a substring of Seymour Twitdum.

The LEFT$ function returns a specified number of characters in a string beginning with the leftmost, or first, character of the string. This is similar to what happens when the hatchet-wielding farmer catches up with his runaway chicken—except cutting a substring from another string is a lot less messy than separating a chicken from its head.

To use LEFT$, you might type a command such as the following:

```
string2$ = LEFT$(string1$, 7)
```

This function call has two arguments. The first argument is the string from which you want to extract a substring; the second argument is the number of characters, counting from the first character in the string, that you want to include in the substring. So, the example

```
string2$ = LEFT$(string1$, 7)
```

returns the first seven characters of the variable string1$. If string1$ was the phrase Yo ho ho and a bottle of rum, LEFT$ would return the string Yo ho h.

The function RIGHT$ returns a specified number of characters in a string starting from the rightmost, or last, character of the string. So, the statement

```
string2$ = RIGHT$(string1$, 7)
```

returns the last seven characters of the variable `string1$`. If `string1$` were the phrase `QBasic is way cool!`, this call to `RIGHT$` would return the string `y cool!`.

Finally, the function `MID$`, which has two forms, allows you to extract text from any position in a string. In fact, you can use `MID$` to do anything you can do with `LEFT$` and `RIGHT$`—and much more. In other words, if you can remember only one string-handling function, `MID$` is the one to remember. If you can't remember even one string-handling function, forget QBasic and join the bikini-gazers at the beach.

In the first form of `MID$`, you supply as arguments the *source string*—the string from which you will cut your substring—and a starting position. The function then returns a substring consisting of all the characters from the starting position to the end of the string. One example is the following program statement:

```
string2$ = MID$(string1$, 7)
```

In this case, if `string1$` was `I'd rather be at the beach`, `string2$` would be equal to `ther be at the beach`. (The *t* in *rather* is the seventh character in `string1$`.)

In the second form of `MID$`, you supply as arguments the source string, a starting position, and the length of the substring you want. The function then returns a string composed of all the characters from the starting position up to the requested length. Assuming that `string1$` still equals `I'd rather be at the beach`, the statement

```
string2$ = MID$(string1$, 7, 4)
```

would make `string2$` equal to `ther`.

TIP

Although LEFT$ and RIGHT$ are handy functions, you can replace any call to them with a call to MID$ (you *call* a function when you use it). For example, the following two function calls produce exactly the same results:

```
string2$ = LEFT$(string1$, 8)
```

and

```
string2$ = MID$(string1$, 1, 8)
```

Likewise, the next two function calls also produce the same results:

```
string2$ = RIGHT$(string1$, 8)
```

and

```
string2$ = MID$(string1$, LEN(string1$)-7)
```

To get a little practice with substrings, try the program in Listing 5.3. When you run the program, you are asked to enter a string. Type anything you like, as long as the text is at least seven characters long and doesn't contain words that make people blush. After you enter the string, the program extracts several substrings and displays them on-screen.

Listing 5.3 STRING1.BAS displays substrings

These lines extract substrings from **string1$**

```
CLS
INPUT "Enter a string: ", string1$
string2$ = LEFT$(string1$, 5)
string3$ = RIGHT$(string1$, 5)
string4$ = MID$(string1$, 3, 5)
```

continues

Listing 5.3 Continued

```
          PRINT
The semicolon ───── PRINT "The first five characters are ";
keeps the          PRINT "'"; string2$; "'"
next printing      PRINT "The last five characters are ";
position on        PRINT "'"; string3$; "'"
the same line      PRINT "Five characters from the middle are ";
          PRINT "'"; string4$; "'"
```

**IN SIMPLE
TERMS**

Listing 5.3 clears the screen, then asks the user to input a
string. The program then takes the user's string, which is
stored in the string variable string1$, and uses the string-
handling functions LEFT$, RIGHT$, and MID$ to extract three
substrings. These substrings are stored in the variables
string2$, string3$, and string4$, respectively. Finally,
after printing a blank line, the program displays the three
substrings.

Here is typical output from Listing 5.3:

```
Enter a string: This is a test.

The first five characters are 'This '
The last five characters are 'test.'
Five characters from the middle are 'is is'
```

Look at the PRINT commands near the end of the program and notice
how some end with a semicolon? When you end a PRINT command with
a semicolon, the next PRINT command following it begins printing on
the same line as the first PRINT command. Because the first PRINT in each
pair of PRINT commands ends with a semicolon, each pair prints only a
single line of text.

NOTE

When you run the program in Listing 5.3, try entering a string that's less than five characters in length. Because the LEFT$ and RIGHT$ string-handling functions assume a string length of at least five characters, and the function MID$ assumes a string length of at least seven characters, you might expect the program to drop dead if you give it a string shorter than it expects. QBasic's functions are smart little devils. If you give them values that don't make sense, they usually can still figure out how to handle the situation. Despite QBasic's cleverness, you should watch out for this kind of error. The following output shows what happens if you enter a string with fewer than five characters:

```
Enter a string: rat

The first five characters are 'rat'
The last five characters are 'rat'
Five characters from the middle are 't'
```

Finding Substrings

(A textual scavenger hunt)

Now that you know how to extract a substring from a larger string, you may wonder how you can find the exact substring you want. Suppose, for example, you have a string containing a list of names, and you want to find the name Twitdum. The function INSTR (which stands for *in string*) was created for just this task. (Well, actually, it was created to find *any* string, not just Twitdum.)

Like the function MID$, INSTR (notice that there's no dollar sign after INSTR) has two forms. One form of INSTR enables you to find the first occurrence of a substring by providing the function with the *source string* (the string to search through) as well as the substring for which to search. For example, the following line finds the position of the substring Twitdum in string1$:

```
P% = INSTR(string1$, "Twitdum")
```

When you find the position of the string, simply use MID$ to extract the actual string. (If INSTR cannot find the requested substring, it returns a value of 0.) In the preceding "Twitdum" example, you'd use MID$ to extract the substring like this:

```
string2$ = MID$(string1$, P%, 7)
```

After finding the first occurrence of a substring, you may want to search the rest of the string for another occurrence. After all, your name list might contain more than one Twitdum. To continue searching, you use the second form of the INSTR function. This second form takes as arguments not only the string to search and the substring for which to search, but also the starting position of the search.

You could use the value returned in P% to continue searching the string, as in the following:

```
P% = INSTR(P% + 1, string1$, "Twitdum")
```

Notice that the starting position, which is the function's first argument, is P% + 1, not just P%. If you used P%, the function would find the same substring it just found. An error like this in your program can be very frustrating and hard to detect.

The program in Listing 5.4 demonstrates how all this substring search stuff works. This program requires no input. Just run it and compare its output with the program listing.

Listing 5.4 FIND1.BAS finds substrings

A list of names ⸻

```
CLS
string1$ = "SmithTwitdumFreemanTwitdumRothTwitdum"
position% = INSTR(string1$, "Twitdum")
PRINT "The first occurrence of ";
PRINT "'"; MID$(string1$, position%, 7); "' ";
PRINT "is at position"; position%
position% = INSTR(position% + 1, string1$, "Twitdum")
PRINT "The second occurrence of ";
PRINT "'"; MID$(string1$, position%, 7); "' ";
PRINT "is at position"; position%
position% = INSTR(position% + 1, string1$, "Twitdum")
PRINT "The third occurrence of ";
PRINT "'"; MID$(string1$, position%, 7); "' ";
PRINT "is at position"; position%
```

INSTR finds the string

You don't have to put an extracted substring ⸻ into a string variable. Just print the function's output

IN SIMPLE TERMS

After clearing the screen, Listing 5.4 sets the string variable string1$ to a list of names. Then the program uses the INSTR function to find the position of the first occurrence of the substring Twitdum, which is stored in the integer variable position%. Three PRINT commands then display the substring and its position, using the MID$ function and the value of position%. Next, the INSTR function finds the position of the second occurrence of the substring—this time using the form of INSTR that specifies the starting position for the search. In this example, the starting position is position% + 1. Again, the PRINT commands display the substring and its position. The third occurrence of the substring is located and displayed in the same way. If the source string contained more than three occurrences of Twitdum, you could find them in exactly the same way that the program found the first three.

Here is the output from the program in Listing 5.4:

```
The first occurrence of 'Twitdum' is at position 6
The second occurrence of 'Twitdum' is at position 20
The third occurrence of 'Twitdum' is at position 31
```

Another way to use the string functions presented in this chapter is to separate words in a string. To do this, you have to know the character between the words. This character, which can be anything you like, is called a *delimiter*. In most sentences, the delimiter is the space character. Listing 5.5 is a program that asks you to type a string containing three words separated by spaces. After you enter the string, the program uses the string-handling functions to find and separate the words into different strings.

BUZZWORD

Delimiter

A *delimiter* is a character used to separate words in a string. For example, the delimiter in the string Fred,Sam,Otis,Hal is a comma.

Listing 5.5 FIND2.BAS uses delimiters to separate a string into substrings

Remember the purpose of the semi-colon at the end of a **PRINT** statement

```
CLS
PRINT "Enter a string containing three ";
PRINT "words separated by spaces."
INPUT string1$
pos1% = INSTR(string1$, " ")
word1$ = LEFT$(string1$, pos1% - 1)
pos2% = INSTR(pos1% + 1, string1$, " ")
word2$ = MID$(string1$, pos1% + 1, pos2% - pos1% - 1)
word3$ = RIGHT$(string1$, LEN(string1$) - pos2%)
PRINT
PRINT "Your three words are ";
PRINT "'"; word1$; ",' '"; word2$; ",' and '"; word3$; ".'"
```

The space character marks the boundary between words

**IN SIMPLE
TERMS**

The first four lines of Listing 5.5 clear the screen, print a prompt, and ask the user to enter a string consisting of three words separated by spaces. In the fifth line of the program, the location of the first space character is found; its position is stored in the integer variable pos1%. In the sixth line, the LEFT$ function is used to extract the first word from the string by using the location of the space minus 1 as the length of the substring. (For example, if the first word in the string is *muskrat*, the first space will be at position 8. The length of *muskrat* is then 8–1, or 7.)

In the seventh line, the location of the second space charac- ter is found, and the eighth line uses the function MID$ to extract the second word from the string. The start of the second word is located at pos1% + 1, which is the position of the first character after the first space. The length of the word is calculated by subtracting the location of the first space from the location of the second space minus one. (If you find these calculations a little confusing, run through each program step on a piece of paper. You'll see that the math is really very simple. It's just difficult to describe in English.)

The program extracts the third word using the RIGHT$ func- tion. The number of characters to extract from the right of the string is calculated by subtracting the position of the second space from the length of the string. Finally, the last three lines of the program print the program's output, which displays the three words that were extracted from the main string.

Here is the output from Listing 5.5:

```
Enter a string containing three words separated by spaces.
? One Two Three

Your three words are 'One,' 'Two,' and 'Three.'
```

Listing 5.5 is the most complicated program you've confronted. Study it carefully to be sure you understand the way the various functions determine the location of each word in the string. Also review how each word is then extracted into a separate string variable. When you understand this program, you're well on your way to being a QBasic programmer.

Please realize that Listing 5.5 isn't nearly as complicated as it may seem from reading its description. Describing even fairly simple programming ideas in English—especially mathematical and logical concepts—often requires lots of words. If you don't understand how Listing 5.5 works, grab a pencil and a piece of paper. Start at the top of the listing and work each program line out on paper. By playing computer and writing the results of each command down in black and white, you'll quickly see how the program works—without words getting in the way.

You can use the techniques you learned in Listing 5.5 to do all sorts of useful things in your programs. You might, for example, want to write a program that counts the number of words in a document. To do this, you would want to look for the spaces that separate words. You could also use string-handling techniques to take a group of words, extract them from a document, and then sort them into alphabetical order. You're not ready to write these kinds of programs yet, of course, but by the time you get to the end of this book, you will be.

Changing Case

(A capital idea)

As you know, alphabetic characters in QBasic can be typed either in uppercase or lowercase letters. Sometimes, you might want your strings to be displayed all in one case or the other. To change all characters in a string to either uppercase or lowercase, use two handy QBasic functions: UCASE$ (which, not too surprisingly, stands for *uppercase*) and LCASE$ (which, you guessed it, stands for *lowercase*).

To see how UCASE$ and LCASE$ work, try the program in Listing 5.6—a revised version of Listing 5.5. If you've already typed Listing 5.5, simply use it again and add the last eight lines of Listing 5.6 to it. Then use the **File** menu's Save **As**... command to save the file under the name FIND3.BAS.

> **Listing 5.6 FIND3.BAS displays substrings in uppercase and lowercase**

```
CLS
PRINT "Enter a string containing three ";
PRINT "words separated by spaces."
INPUT string1$
pos1% = INSTR(string1$, " ")
word1$ = LEFT$(string1$, pos1% - 1)
pos2% = INSTR(pos1% + 1, string1$, " ")
word2$ = MID$(string1$, pos1% + 1, pos2% - pos1% - 1)
word3$ = RIGHT$(string1$, LEN(string1$) - pos2%)
PRINT
PRINT "Your three words are ";
PRINT "'"; word1$; ",' '"; word2$; ",' and '"; word3$; ".'"
```

continues

Listing 5.6 Continued

Here's where the program lowercases the strings. The colon lets you put more than one statement on a line.

```
word1$ = UCASE$(word1$): word2$ = UCASE$(word2$)
word3$ = UCASE$(word3$)
PRINT "Your three words in uppercase are ";
PRINT "'"; word1$; ",' '"; word2$; ",' and '"; word3$; ".'"
word1$ = LCASE$(word1$): word2$ = LCASE$(word2$)
word3$ = LCASE$(word3$)
PRINT "Your three words in lowercase are ";
PRINT "'"; word1$; ",' '"; word2$; ",' and '"; word3$; ".'"
```

Here's where the program uppercases the strings

The punctuation in this line is confusing. Study it carefully.

IN SIMPLE TERMS

Listing 5.6 is identical to Listing 5.5, except for the last eight lines. The first four new lines convert the three substrings to uppercase and display them. The last four lines convert the substrings to lowercase and display them.

When you run FIND3.BAS, be sure the three words in the string you type include both uppercase and lowercase letters. After you type the string, the program displays the three words the way you typed them, followed by the same words in uppercase and then lowercase letters. The following is the output for Listing 5.6:

```
Enter a string containing three words separated by spaces.
? Tom Dick Harry

Your three words are 'Tom,' 'Dick,' and 'Harry.'
Your three words in uppercase are 'TOM,' 'DICK,' and 'HARRY.'
Your three words in lowercase are 'tom,' 'dick,' and 'harry.'
```

TIP

One point of interest in Listing 5.6 is in the line

```
word1$ = UCASE$(word1$): word2$ = UCASE$(word2$)
```

This line demonstrates how you can save space by putting short statements together on a single line, separating them with a colon. However, as handy as this technique may be, you should not overuse it; it may make your programs hard to read. Place multiple statements on a single line only when they are short and closely related in some way.

Converting Numbers to Strings

(And vice versa)

You probably remember that there's a big difference between numerical values and text strings, even if the text string contains numeric characters. Numerical values, such as the number 5 or the integer variable number%, can be used in mathematical operations. Strings, however, cannot. Luckily, QBasic includes a handy function, VAL (which stands for *value*), that lets you convert number strings into numerical values that can be used in mathematical operations. You can also change numerical values into strings with the STR$ function—something you might want to do with the result of a calculation. (*STR*, by the way, is short for *string*.)

To convert a number string into a numerical value, use the VAL function like this:

```
number = VAL(string1$)
```

The variable `string1$` is the string you want to convert to a numerical value. Keep in mind that VAL can convert only string characters that represent numbers: digits, decimal points, and minus signs. The following statement makes `number!` equal to 3.4:

```
number! = VAL("3.4Apples")
```

Because the characters that compose the word `Apples` are not numerical characters, VAL can do nothing with them and ignores them. If VAL cannot convert the string at all, as in the case of

```
number! = VAL("Apples")
```

it returns a value of 0.

You should also know that VAL ignores spaces in strings, and that it understands number strings in scientific notation form. The following table shows a summary of the results of the VAL function when it is used with different strings. (If you don't know about scientific notation, don't worry. Just be aware that the last example in the table shows a string using this number form.)

Function Call	Result
VAL("34")	34
VAL("56.23")	56.23
VAL("23.6&HYG")	23.6
VAL("2 3 4")	234
VAL("-76")	-76
VAL("764,345")	764
VAL("0")	0

Function Call	Result
VAL("SJuHGd")	0
VAL("HFGYR345")	0
VAL("nine")	0
VAL("3.4D+4")	34000

CAUTION

The fact that VAL returns a 0 when it cannot convert a string to a numerical value can lead to problems in your programs. Problems arise because 0 is a perfectly valid numerical value. For example, both of the expressions number = VAL("0") and number = VAL("Apples") return a value of 0; the value is really only valid, however, for the first example. Be aware of this possible ambiguous outcome when using VAL in your programs.

Converting strings to numerical values is only half the story. You may also need to go the other way and convert a numerical variable into a string. You might, for example, want to convert a numerical value to a string so that you can add it to a text document. You can do this conversion by calling the STR$ function, which looks like this: string1$ = STR$(number). Here, number is the numerical value you want to change into string form. For example, the program statement string1$ = STR$(34.45) makes string1$ equal to the string 34.45.

QBASIC FOR ROOKIES

NOTE

When the function STR$ converts a numerical value into a string, it always reserves a space for the value's sign. Strings created from positive numbers always have a leading space, and strings created from negative numbers always begin with a minus sign.

The program in Listing 5.7 demonstrates the VAL and STR$ functions. When you run the program, it requests two numbers that are input as strings. The strings are converted into numerical values so they can be used in an addition operation. The result of this operation, a numerical value, is converted into a string before it's printed.

Listing 5.7 NUMBERS.BAS converts numbers and strings

VAL converts a number string into a numerical value

The result of the mathematical operation can be converted back to a string

```
CLS
INPUT "Enter the first number: ", number1$
INPUT "Enter the second number: ", number2$
number1 = VAL(number1$)
number2 = VAL(number2$)
number3 = number1 + number2
result$ = STR$(number3)
PRINT
PRINT "The result of summing ";
PRINT number1$; " and "; number2$;
PRINT " is"; result$; "."
```

Those converted values can be used in mathematical operations

IN SIMPLE TERMS

Listing 5.7 clears the screen and requests two string values from the user. These strings are stored in the string variables number1$ and number2$. After the strings are entered, the VAL function converts them into numerical values that are stored in the variables number1 and number2. The two values are then added, and the result is stored in the variable

number3. Next, the STR$ function converts the numerical value in number3 to the string result$. Finally, the last few lines print a message to the user, displaying the string in result$.

When you run NUMBERS.BAS, make sure the strings you enter are composed of valid number characters. Otherwise, the program may print incorrect results. The following lines show the output from Listing 5.7:

```
Enter the first number: 23.5
Enter the second number: 65.23

The result of summing 23.5 and 65.23 is 88.73.
```

Common Rookie Mistakes

Formatting strings improperly. When concatenating strings, it's easy to forget that you might need to separate the strings with some sort of delimiter. For example, when joining a first name to a last name, you'll end up with a string like GaryGilbert if you forget to add a space between the two names.

Assuming a specific string length. As you saw in the second output example for Listing 5.3 (in which a string with fewer than five characters was entered), you must be careful when you make assumptions about a string's length. This fact is particularly important to remember when the string is being entered by the user.

Using a QBasic keyword or function name as a variable name. If you get strange syntax errors in your program, check the line in question for invalid variable names. You might think string$ makes a perfectly good

string name, but QBasic will complain vociferously because STRING$ is the name of a QBasic function. (Turn to the inside back cover for a handy quick reference of keywords, functions, and procedures that you've learned about in this book.)

Placing function arguments in the wrong order: When you call a function such as LEFT$, be certain that you have the function's arguments in the right order. A function call such as s$ = LEFT$(n$, 5) works just fine, but the function call s$ = LEFT$(5, n$) stops a QBasic program dead in its tracks.

Summing Up

▼ You can use the plus sign (+) to join strings together. This process is called concatenation.

▼ The equal sign (=) can be used with strings just as it is used with numerical values. Specifically, you use the assignment operator to set a string variable to a specific string value.

▼ The length of a string is the number of characters contained in the string. A null string contains no characters and so has a length of 0.

▼ The LEN function returns, as a numerical value, the length of a string.

▼ A substring is a portion of a larger string.

▼ The functions LEFT$, RIGHT$, and MID$ allow you to extract substrings from other strings.

▼ The function INSTR returns the position of a substring within a string.

▼ You can use the functions LCASE$ and UCASE$ to convert strings to lowercase and uppercase, respectively.

▼ The function VAL converts number strings to numerical values. The function STR$ does the opposite, converting numerical values to strings.

Armed with the knowledge you've gained in the first five chapters of this book, you're now ready to learn the techniques you need to create full-fledged programs. In Chapter 6, you'll learn how computers make decisions—an important part of what makes programs work.

CHAPTER 6

Making Decisions
(Or How to Really Put Your Computer to Work)

IN A NUTSHELL

▼ Using branching to change program flow
▼ Learning about IF, ELSE, and ELSEIF
▼ Understanding relational operators
▼ Working with logical operators

CHAPTER 6

In previous chapters, you learned much about the way QBasic works. You now know how to type programs, how to input and output data, how to perform mathematical operations, and how to handle strings. But these techniques are merely the building blocks of a program. To use these building blocks in a useful way, you have to understand how computers make decisions.

In this chapter, you learn how your programs can analyze data in order to decide what parts of your program to execute. Until now, your programs have executed their statements in strict sequential order, starting with the first line and working, line by line, to the end of the program. Now it's time to learn how you can control your program's flow—the order in which the statements are executed—so that you can do different things based on the data your program receives.

BUZZWORD

> **Program Flow**
>
> *Program flow* is the order in which a program executes its statements. Most program flow is sequential, meaning that the statements are executed one by one in the order in which they appear in the program. However, there are QBasic commands that make your program jump forward or backward, skipping over program code not currently required. These commands are said to control the program flow.

If the idea of computers making decisions based on data seems a little strange, think about how you make decisions. For example, suppose you're expecting an important letter. You go out to your mailbox and look inside. Then you choose one of the following two actions:

▼ If there's mail in the mailbox, you take it into the house.

▼ If there's no mail in the mailbox, you complain about the postal system.

In either case, you've made a decision based on whether or not there is mail in the mailbox.

Computers use this same method to make decisions (except that they never complain and they don't give a darn how late your mail is). You will see the word *if* used frequently in computer programs. Just as you might say to yourself, "If the mail is in the mailbox, I'll bring it in," so a computer uses *if* to decide what action to take.

Program Flow and Branching

(A digital road map)

Program flow is the order in which a program executes its code. Your programs so far in this book have had sequential program flow. Truth is, almost all program code executes sequentially. However, virtually every program reaches a point where a decision must be made about a piece of data. The program must then analyze the data, decide what to do about it, and jump to the appropriate section of code. This decision-making process is as important to computer programming as pollen is to a bee. Virtually no useful programs can be written without it.

When a program breaks the sequential flow and jumps to a new section of code, it is called *branching*. When this branching is based on a decision, the program is performing *conditional branching*. When no decision-making is involved, and the program always branches when it encounters a branching instruction, the program is performing *unconditional branching*.

To continue with the mailbox example, suppose you went out to the mailbox and found your mail, but decided to complain about the Post Office anyway. Because the poor mail carrier was destined to be the

focus of your wrath, whether or not the mail was delivered on time, your complaining is unconditional. No matter what, after going to the mail box, you complain.

Conditional and Unconditional Branching

Unconditional branching occurs when a program branches to a new location in the code without analyzing data and making a decision. An unconditional branch occurs every time your program encounters the branch instruction. Conditional branching occurs when the program branches based on a decision of some type. This type of branching may or may not occur based on the results of the decision.

The *IF-THEN* Statement

(It's simply a matter of choice)

Most conditional branching occurs when the program executes an IF–THEN statement, which compares data and decides what to do next based on the result of the comparison. If the comparison works out one way, the program performs the statement following the THEN keyword. Otherwise, the program does nothing and drops to the next program line. This gives each comparison two possible outcomes.

For example, you've probably seen programs that print menus on the screen. To select a menu item, you often type its selection number. When the program receives your input, it checks the number you entered and decides what to do. Listing 6.1 displays a program that illustrates how this type of menu selection might work.

Listing 6.1 MENU1.BAS is a simple menu program

```
CLS
PRINT
PRINT "    MENU"          ─┐
PRINT "-----------"        │      These statements print
PRINT " 1. Red"           ─┤──── a menu on-screen
PRINT " 2. Green"          │
PRINT " 3. Blue"          ─┘
PRINT
INPUT "Your selection: ", choice%
PRINT
IF choice% = 1 THEN PRINT "You chose red."    ─┐     IF-THEN state-
IF choice% = 2 THEN PRINT "You chose green."   │──── ments determine
IF choice% = 3 THEN PRINT "You chose blue."   ─┘     the menu selec-
                                                     tion chosen
```

IN SIMPLE TERMS

After clearing the screen, the program in Listing 6.1 displays a menu. Using an INPUT statement, the program asks the user to enter a menu selection that is then stored in the numerical variable choice%. The last three lines of the program check the value of choice% and print an appropriate message if the user entered a valid menu selection.

Here's the output for Listing 6.1:

```
    MENU
-----------
 1. Red
 2. Green
 3. Blue

Your selection: 2

You chose green.
```

The preceding program prints a menu and lets you enter a menu selection. The program then uses a series of IF–THEN statements to compare the value you entered with the acceptable menu choices. See the equal signs in the IF–THEN statements? These are not assignment operators; they are *relational operators* that enable you to compare two or more values. Look at the first IF–THEN statement in the program. If this line were written in English, it would read "If the value of the variable choice% equals 1, then print...." The other IF–THEN statements in the program have similar meanings.

BUZZWORD

Relational Operators

Relational operators, such as the equal sign, enable you to compare two pieces of data. By comparing variables to constants, for example, you can check variables for specific values. The most common relational operator is the equal sign, which checks whether two expressions are equal. However, there are also relational operators for such relationships as *less than*, *greater than*, and *not equal*. (You'll see these operators later in this chapter.) When you use relational operators to compare two values, you are writing a *conditional expression*, which is an expression that is either true or false.

A simple IF–THEN statement includes the keyword IF followed by a *Boolean expression*—an expression that evaluates to either true or false. You follow the Boolean expression with the keyword THEN and, finally, with the statement that you want executed if the Boolean expression is true.

QBASIC FOR ROOKIES

PLAY BALL!

BUZZWORD

Boolean Expression

A *Boolean expression* is an expression that evaluates to either true or false. For example, the expression 3+4=7 is true, whereas the expression 6+1=9 is false. A Boolean expression usually compares a variable to a constant or to another variable, such as num+1=7 or num1-10=num2.

How do IF—THEN statements work? Let's say that when you execute the program in Listing 6.1, you type the value 1. When the program gets to the first IF—THEN statement, it checks the value of choice%. If choice% equals 1 (which it does, in this case), the program prints the message You chose red and then drops down to the next IF—THEN statement. This time, the program compares the value of choice% with the number 2. Because choice% doesn't equal 2, the program ignores the THEN part of the statement and drops down to the next program line, which is another IF—THEN statement. The variable choice% doesn't equal 3 either, so the THEN portion of the third IF—THEN statement is also ignored. The program ends at this point because there are no more program lines left.

Suppose you enter the number 2 at the menu. When the program gets to the first IF—THEN statement, it discovers that choice% is not equal to 1, so it ignores the THEN part of the statement and drops down to the next program line, which is the second IF—THEN statement. Again, the program checks the value of choice%. Because choice% equals 2, the program can execute the THEN portion of the statement; the message You chose green is printed on-screen. Program execution drops down to the third IF—THEN statement, which does nothing because choice% doesn't equal 3.

NOTE

The conditional expression in an IF—THEN statement, no matter how complex, always evaluates to either true or false. If the expression evaluates to true, the THEN portion of the statement is executed. If the expression evaluates to false, the THEN portion is not executed. True and false are actual values: true equals any nonzero value, and false equals 0. Consequently, the statement IF 1 THEN PRINT "True!" prints the message True!; but the statement IF 0 THEN PRINT "False!" does nothing. In the first statement, the value 1 is considered true, so the THEN part of the statement is executed. In the second statement, the 0 is considered false, so the THEN portion of the statement is ignored.

Multi-Line *IF-THEN* Statements

(Lots of choices)

Listing 6.1 demonstrates the simplest IF—THEN statement. This simple statement usually fits your program's decision-making needs just fine. Sometimes, however, you want to perform more than one command as part of an IF—THEN statement. To perform more than one command, press Enter after THEN, write the commands you want to add to the IF—THEN statement, and end the block of commands with the END IF keyword. Listing 6.2 uses this technique and is a revised version of the MENU program from Listing 6.1.

Listing 6.2 MENU2.BAS is a color version of the menu program

```
CLS
PRINT
PRINT "    MENU"
PRINT "-----------"
PRINT " 1. Red"
PRINT " 2. Green"
PRINT " 3. Blue"
PRINT
INPUT "Your selection: ", choice%
PRINT

IF choice% = 1 THEN
  COLOR 4
  PRINT "You chose red."
END IF                                    Use END IF to create
                                          multi-line IF statements

IF choice% = 2 THEN
  COLOR 2
  PRINT "You chose green."                Each menu choice changes
END IF                                    the color of the text

IF choice% = 3 THEN
  COLOR 1
  PRINT "You chose blue."
END IF

COLOR 7                                   This line changes text
                                          back to white
```

**IN SIMPLE
TERMS**

Listing 6.2 is similar to Listing 6.1. The primary difference is
that the program prints the message in the chosen color,
rather than in boring white text. First, the program clears the
screen and prints the menu and then requests the user's

continues

continued

menu selection. Next, the three IF—THEN statements compare the user's selection with the possible menu choices. When an IF—THEN statement's conditional expression evaluates to true, the program lines between the IF and the next END IF (which change the text color and print the message) are executed. Only one IF—THEN statement can possibly evaluate to true, so no more than one message can ever be printed. The last COLOR statement in the program returns the text color to white.

The output for the program in Listing 6.2 looks like this:

```
    MENU
- - - - - - - - - - -
  1. Red
  2. Green
  3. Blue

Your selection: 1

You chose red.
```

TIP

Notice that some program lines in Listing 6.2 are indented. By indenting the lines that go with each IF block, you can more easily see the structure of your program. Listing 6.2 also uses blank lines to separate blocks of code that go together. The computer doesn't care about the indenting or the blank lines, but these features make your programs easier for you, or another programmer, to read.

What's happening in Listing 6.2? Suppose you run the program and enter the number 2. When the program gets to the first IF–THEN statement, it compares the value of choice% with the number 1. Because these values don't match (or, in programmer lingo, the statement doesn't evaluate to true), the program skips over every program line until it finds an END IF statement, which marks the end of the block of code that goes with the IF.

This brings the program to the second IF–THEN statement. When the program evaluates the conditional expression, it finds that choice% equals 2, and it executes the THEN portion of the IF–THEN statement. This time the THEN portion is not just one command, but two. The program changes the text color to green (the color selected from the menu) and then prints the message. Finally, the program reaches END IF, which marks the end of the IF–THEN statement.

This brings the program to the last IF–THEN statement, which the program skips over because choice% doesn't equal 3. The last line of the program is a COLOR statement without an IF. This command changes the text back to its original white color.

NOTE

When you want to set up a multi-line IF statement, you must end the first program line of the statement after THEN. This is the signal to QBasic that all the following commands, up to the next END IF, are part of the IF block.

You might think it's a waste of time for the program to evaluate other IF–THEN statements after it finds a match for the menu item you chose. You'd be right, too. When you write programs, you should always look for ways to make them run faster. One way to make a program run faster is to avoid all unnecessary processing. But how, you may ask, do you avoid unnecessary processing when you have to compare a variable with more than one value?

QBASIC FOR ROOKIES

One way to keep processing to a minimum is to use QBasic's ELSEIF clause. Before you learn about ELSEIF, however, let's look at the simpler version, ELSE. This keyword enables you to use a single IF–THEN statement to choose between two outcomes. When the IF–THEN statement evaluates to true, the THEN part of the statement is executed. When the IF–THEN statement evaluates to false, the ELSE portion is executed. When the IF–ELSE statement evaluates to neither true nor false, it's time to get a new computer. Listing 6.3 demonstrates how ELSEIF works.

Listing 6.3 HELLO1.BAS recognizes the name of its user

```
CLS
INPUT "Please enter your name: ", name$
PRINT
IF name$ = "Fred" THEN ───────────── You can compare
    PRINT "Hi, Fred!"                 strings, too
ELSE ──────────────────────────── ELSE enables an IF–THEN
    PRINT "Hello, stranger."          statement to associate
END IF                                program code to each of
                                      two outcomes
```

IN SIMPLE TERMS

Listing 6.3 clears the screen and then asks the user for his name. If the user types *Fred*, the program prints the message Hi, Fred!. Then, skipping over the ELSE clause, the program drops down to the END IF. If the user types something other than *Fred*, the program skips the THEN portion of the IF–THEN statement and instead prints the message Hello, stranger.

Here is the output for Listing 6.3:

```
Please enter your name: Fred

Hi, Fred!
```

When you run this program, you're asked to enter your name. If you enter the name *Fred*, the program recognizes you and gives you a personal hello. Otherwise, the program considers you a stranger and treats you accordingly. (If you like, you can personalize the program by changing all occurrences of *Fred* to your name.) As you can see, the ELSE clause is executed only when the IF–THEN statement is false. If the IF–THEN statement is true, the program ignores the ELSE clause.

The program in Listing 6.3 also demonstrates how to compare strings. Strings are compared just as numerical values are: by using the equal sign, which, in the case of an IF–THEN statement, is a relational operator. You will compare strings often in your programs, especially programs that require text input from the user. By using string comparisons, you can catch an incorrect response to a prompt and print an error message on-screen to inform the user of the incorrect entry.

ELSE provides a default outcome for an IF–THEN statement. A default outcome doesn't help much, however, in an IF–THEN statement that must associate program code with more than two possible outcomes (as in the previous menu program). Suppose you want Listing 6.3 to recognize your friends' names, too. No problem. First, get some friends; then use QBasic's ELSEIF keyword, as shown in Listing 6.4.

Listing 6.4 HELLO2.BAS recognizes three different users

```
CLS
INPUT "Please enter your name: ", name$
PRINT
name$ = UCASE$(name$)
IF name$ = "FRED" THEN
   PRINT "Hi, Fred!"
ELSEIF name$ = "SARAH" THEN
   PRINT "How's it going, Sarah?"
ELSEIF name$ = "TONY" THEN
   PRINT "Hey! It's my man Tony!"
ELSE
   PRINT "Hello, stranger."
END IF
```

Using uppercase for a string makes it easier to use in a comparison

ELSEIF clauses allow **IF–THEN** statements to handle many outcomes

QBASIC FOR ROOKIES

IN SIMPLE TERMS

Listing 6.4 first clears the screen. Then it asks for the user's name, which the program changes to all uppercase letters. Next, the IF–THEN statement checks for the name FRED. If the user entered FRED, the program prints Fred's message. Otherwise, the ELSEIF clauses check for other names and print an appropriate message if a match is found. If none of the names match the user's input, the ELSE clause executes and prints a generic message on the screen.

The output for Listing 6.4 looks like this:

```
Please enter your name: sarah

How's it going, Sarah?
```

TIP

When you need to get string input from the user, as in Listing 6.4, it's often a good idea to change the input to all upper- or lowercase. This enables the program to recognize a word no matter in which case the user types it. For example, in Listing 6.4, the user's input is modified to uppercase before it is compared to the names in the IF and ELSEIF clauses. With this method, Fred can type his name any way he likes: Fred, fred, FRED, or even fRed. One of your goals as a programmer should be to make your programs as easy to use as possible. Allowing the user to enter a string in any form is one way to do this.

In Listing 6.4, as in Listing 6.3, you're asked to enter a name. But this time, the program uses an IF–THEN statement with a series of ELSEIF clauses to check the name entered against the names the program can

recognize. When the program finds a match, it skips over any remaining ELSEIF and ELSE clauses. If the program finds no match—that is, the user hasn't entered the name *Fred*, *Sarah*, or *Tony*—the ELSE clause executes and provides a default response. This default ensures that, no matter what the user types, he or she will receive a greeting.

Listing 6.5 is a new version of the menu program that uses ELSEIF and ELSE clauses. You should now know enough about computer decision-making to figure out how it works.

Listing 6.5 MENU3.BAS runs more efficiently than previous versions of the program

```
CLS
PRINT
PRINT "    MENU"
PRINT "-----------"
PRINT " 1. Red"
PRINT " 2. Green"
PRINT " 3. Blue"
PRINT
INPUT "Your selection: ", choice%
PRINT

IF choice% = 1 THEN
  COLOR 4
  PRINT "You chose red."
ELSEIF choice% = 2 THEN
  COLOR 2
  PRINT "You chose green."
ELSEIF choice% = 3 THEN
  COLOR 1
  PRINT "You chose blue."
ELSE
  PRINT "Invalid selection!"
END IF

COLOR 7
```

A series of **ELSEIF** clauses are faster than using many **IFs**

The **ELSE** clause allows for a default response

IN SIMPLE TERMS

Listing 6.5, as always, first clears the screen and prints a menu. It then asks the user to enter a menu selection. The IF–THEN statement compares the user's input with the acceptable menu values. If it finds a match, the program changes the text color to the selected color and prints a message. If it finds no match, the program displays an error message.

Here's the output for Listing 6.5:

```
        MENU
 - - - - - - - - - - -
   1. Red
   2. Green
   3. Blue

Your selection: 2

You chose green.
```

Relational Operators

(How do you compare?)

The previous programs in this chapter used only the equals operator to compare values. Often you'll need to compare values in other ways. You might, for example, want to know if a value is less than or greater than another value. QBasic features an entire set of relational operators you can use in IF–THEN statements and in other types of comparisons. These operators include not only the equal sign (=), but also not equal to (<>), less than (<), greater than (>), less than or equal (<=), and greater than or equal (>=). The relational operators are summarized in the following table.

Operator	Meaning	Examples
=	Equals	3=(4-1) or "FRED"="FRED"
<>	Not equal	5<>(3+3) or "FRED"<>"SAM"
<	Less than	3<23 or "A"<"B"
>	Greater than	41>39 or "BART">"ADAM"
<=	Less than or equal	5<=6 or "ONE"<="ONE"
>=	Greater than or equal	10>=10 or "THREE">="TWO"

Listing 6.6 demonstrates the use of the less-than operator.

Listing 6.6 NUMRNGE1.BAS determines the size of a number

Relational operators let you check for many types of relationships between data

```
CLS
INPUT "Enter a number no larger than 50: ", number
PRINT
IF number < 10 THEN
   PRINT "Your number is less than 10."
ELSEIF number < 20 THEN
   PRINT "Your number is greater than 9 and less than 20."
ELSEIF number < 30 THEN
   PRINT "Your number is greater than 19 and less than 30."
ELSEIF number < 40 THEN
   PRINT "Your number is greater than 29 and less than 40."
ELSEIF number < 50 THEN
   PRINT "Your number is greater than 39 and less than 50."
ELSEIF number = 50 THEN
   PRINT "Your number is 50."
```

continues

Listing 6.6 Continued

```
ELSE
    PRINT "Your number is out of the acceptable range."
END IF ──────────────────────────────── Every multi-line IF–THEN statement
                                         must end with an END IF
```

**IN SIMPLE
TERMS**

After clearing the screen, Listing 6.6 asks the user to enter a number no greater than 50. After the user types the number, the program uses an IF–THEN statement with a series of ELSEIF clauses to determine the range within which the number falls. For this determination, the program uses the less-than operator (<). If the selected number is less than the numerical constant in the IF or ELSEIF clauses, the program prints an appropriate message to the user. If the number is larger than the constant, the program moves on to the next clause and again makes the comparison, this time with a higher numerical constant. Finally, if the number turns out to be larger than the allowed maximum of 50, the program prints an error message.

The output for Listing 6.6 looks like this:

```
Enter a number no larger than 50: 60

Your number is out of the acceptable range.
```

When you run the program shown in Listing 6.6, the program asks that you enter a number no larger than 50. After you type the number, the program determines the number's range and prints a message informing you of this range. This program doesn't just demonstrate the use of the less-than operator; it keeps you off the streets by having you do a lot of typing. More importantly, Listing 6.6 illustrates the way a block of IF and ELSEIF clauses work.

Suppose when you run the program in Listing 6.6, you type the number 9. When the program gets to the IF clause, it compares 9 to 10 and discovers that 9 is less than 10. (And to think you paid hundreds of dollars for a machine to tell you that.) The IF clause then evaluates to true and the program prints the message `Your number is less than 10`.

Look at the block of ELSEIFs that go along with the IF. Isn't 9 also less than 20? Moreover, isn't 9 also less than 30, 40, and 50? Why then, when you enter the number 9, don't you also see the messages associated with all of these ELSEIFs, as well as the message associated with the IF? And why, when you drop a piece of buttered bread, does it always land butter-side down? (Just thought I'd ask.)

The answer to the first question has to do with the way the IF—ELSEIF block works. (The answer to the second question will never be known, so we'll just ignore it.) After an IF or ELSEIF evaluates to true, the program skips the rest of the statements in the block—or, as programmers say, the program branches to the next statement after the block. In the case of Listing 6.6, there is no statement after the block so the program simply ends.

NOTE

When using relational operators with strings, the value of each letter in a string is relative to its alphabetic order. In other words, the letter A is less than the letter B, the letter B is less than the letter C, and so on. When comparing lowercase letters and uppercase letters, however, the lowercase letters have a greater value than their uppercase counterparts. Therefore, a is greater than A, and b is greater than B. Finally, just as when you organize words into alphabetical order, when a program compares strings, the letters on the left have greater significance than those on the right. For example, Mick is less than Mike to QBasic.

QBASIC FOR ROOKIES

Logical Operators

(Your computer as Spock)

A single comparison in an IF–THEN statement often isn't enough to determine whether data matches your criteria. How can you be sure, for example, that the user enters a number within a specific range? You could hold a gun to the user's head as he's typing the data. Although this may ensure that data is entered properly, it requires that you stay by the computer at all times. Hardly practical. A better way to ensure that data is in the correct range is to use logical operators in your IF–THEN statements.

Let's say that the user is asked to enter a number between 10 and 50, inclusive. To discover whether a number is within this range, you must check not only that the number is greater than or equal to 10, but also that the number is less than or equal to 50. To help handle these situations, QBasic features three logical operators—AND, OR, and NOT—that can be used to combine expressions in an IF statement.

PLAY BALL!

BUZZWORD

Logical Operators

Logical operators, including AND, OR, and NOT, enable you to evaluate more than one condition in a single IF statement. They're called logical operators because they use computer logic to join two or more Boolean expressions into a larger Boolean expression. (Remember, Boolean expressions always evaluate to true or false.)

The AND operator requires all expressions to be true in order for the entire expression to be true. For example, the expression (3+2=5) AND (6+2=8) is true because the expressions on both sides of the AND are true.

However, the expression `(4+3=9) AND (3+3=6)` is not true, because the expression on the left of the `AND` is not true. Remember this when combining expressions with `AND`: if any expression is false, the entire expression is false.

The `OR` operator requires only one expression to be true in order for the entire expression to be true. For example, the expressions `(3+6=2) OR (4+4=8)` and `(4+1=5) OR (7+2=9)` are both true because at least one of the expressions being compared is true. Note that in the second case both expressions being compared are true, which also makes an `OR` expression true.

The `NOT` operator switches the value of (or negates) a logical expression. For example, the expression `(4+3=5)` is not true; however, the expression `NOT (4+3=5)` is true. Take a look at the following expression:

```
(4+5=9) AND NOT (3+1=3)
```

Is this expression true or false? If you said true, you understand the way the logical operators work. The expressions on either side of the `AND` are both true, so the entire expression is true. If you said false, you must go to bed without any dinner.

Of course, you wouldn't write expressions like `(4+5=9) AND NOT (3+1=3)` in your programs. They would serve no purpose because you already know how the expressions evaluate. However, when you use variables, you have no way of knowing in advance how an expression may evaluate. For example, is the expression `(num < 9) AND (num > 15)` true or false? You don't know without being told the value of the numerical variable `num`. By using these logical operators in your `IF—THEN` statements, though, your program can do the evaluation, and, based on the result—true or false—take the appropriate action.

Listing 6.7 demonstrates how logical operators work. When you run the program, it asks you to enter a number between 10 and 50. If you type a number that is out of that range, the program lets you know. Although Listing 6.7 is similar to Listing 6.6, it works very differently. After the user types a number, the program uses a single IF–THEN statement to determine whether the number is within the acceptable range. If the number is out of range, the program prints an error message and ends.

Listing 6.7 NUMRNGE2.BAS stops the program when it discovers improper input

```
CLS
INPUT "Enter a number between 10 and 50: ", number
PRINT
IF (number < 10) OR (number > 50) THEN————————
    PRINT "The number"; number; "is out of range!"
ELSE
    PRINT "The number"; number; "is in range."
END IF
```

Logical operators permit many comparisons with a single **IF** statement

IN SIMPLE TERMS

After clearing the screen, Listing 6.7 asks the user to enter a number between 10 and 50. The program then compares the number entered with the constants 10 and 50. If the number is less than 10 or greater than 50, the program prints an error message and ends. Otherwise, program execution branches to the ELSE clause, which results in a different message being printed on-screen.

The output for Listing 6.7 looks like this:

```
Enter a number between 10 and 50: 35

The number 35 is in range.
```

The Infamous *GOTO*

Most of this chapter has been dedicated to conditional branches. If you recall, however, programmers can also use unconditional branches. This type of branching can be accomplished by using the GOTO instruction, which forces program execution to branch to a specific line number or label. Because line numbers in BASIC programs are now obsolete, you don't have to worry about how to use them—you never will need them. You may, however, want to use labels (although even that is unlikely).

Listing 6.8 is a QBasic program that uses the GOTO instruction to branch to a specific place in the program. The destination of the branch is marked by the label lessthan.

Listing 6.8 GOTO.BAS demonstrates the GOTO command

```
CLS
INPUT "Please enter a number: ", number
PRINT
IF number <= 100 THEN GOTO lessthan ——————— The GOTO statement is
PRINT "Your number is greater than 100."        seldom used in modern
END                                             programs
lessthan:
PRINT "Your number is less than or equal to 100."
```

**IN SIMPLE
TERMS**

After clearing the screen, Listing 6.8 uses an INPUT statement to get a number from the user. Next, the IF—THEN statement checks whether the number is less than or equal to 100. If it is, the THEN portion of the statement, which is a GOTO statement, is executed. GOTO sends program execution to the

continues

QBASIC FOR ROOKIES

continued

label `lessthan`, at which point the program prints an appropriate message and ends. If the number the user enters is greater than 100, the IF–THEN statement's conditional expression evaluates to false. In this case, program execution drops down to the next line, the program prints a message, and the END statement ends the program.

Here is the output for Listing 6.8:

```
Please enter a number: 132

Your number is greater than 100.
```

In Listing 6.8, notice that when the label's name follows the GOTO, it doesn't include a colon; however, the actual label in the program does include a colon. Notice also that this program uses the command END to stop the program's execution. You haven't seen this command before. Although it is not often used in programs, there may be times when you find it useful. Since the END statement is a command just like PRINT or INPUT, you can have as many as you like in a program. After all, there might be more than one place in your program where you need to stop program execution. As you can see in Listing 6.8, the END keyword doesn't mark the actual end of the program. Rather, it tells QBasic to stop executing statements.

NOTE

Although the GOTO statement may seem like a handy thing to have around, it has been so misused in the past that most programmers avoid it like nuclear waste. Overuse of GOTO can turn a program into a tangled, unreadable mess. A modern, structured language like QBasic has no need for the GOTO

instruction. It is included in QBasic only to keep the language compatible with earlier versions of BASIC. This is the last time you will see the GOTO instruction in this book. Start developing good habits now and never use GOTO in your programs.

As soon as you understand all this stuff about computer decision-making, you'll be 90 percent of the way to becoming a QBasic programmer. Making decisions is, after all, one of the most important things a program does. It's safe to say that there's not a single worthwhile program on the planet that doesn't use IF–THEN statements or something similar.

Common Rookie Mistakes

Backward logic. Often, an IF–THEN statement that contains several expressions joined by logical operators is confusing to understand. It is sometimes necessary to add parentheses not only to organize the expressions, but also to be sure that the expressions are evaluated in the proper order. For example, look at the following IF–THEN statement:

```
IF ((num > 10) AND (num < 20)) OR (NOT CHOICE) THEN...
```

Because expressions inside parentheses are evaluated first, the outermost parentheses around the ANDed expressions ensure that the AND is evaluated before the OR. In addition, expressions with parentheses are evaluated from the inside out. In other words, num>10 and num<20 are evaluated before the AND, and the AND is evaluated before the OR. Without the extra parentheses in the preceding IF–THEN statement, you wouldn't know which expressions went with the AND and which went with the OR.

Unexpected values in input. Remember that when you use an INPUT statement, the user can type virtually anything. It's up to your program to ensure that the value entered is appropriate for the program. For this reason, adding an ELSE clause to an IF–THEN statement is a good idea. It ensures that every possible value gets a response from the program.

Confusing the less-than and greater-than operators. Because the less-than operator (<) and the greater-than operator (>) look so much alike, it's easy to get them confused. There's a trick to help you learn which is which: The small side of the operator (the point) always points to the smaller value and the large side of the operator always points to the larger value.

Overusing GOTO. The GOTO statement was important when the BASIC computer language was first invented. Now, however, there's no need to use it in most programs. This book included a brief discussion on GOTO only because you will see GOTO in other programs, so you should know how it works.

Summing Up

▼ Program flow is the order in which a program executes its statements.

▼ When a computer program branches, it jumps to a new location in the code and continues execution from there.

▼ An IF–THEN statement compares the values of data and decides what statements to execute based on that evaluation.

▼ The ELSE and ELSEIF clauses allow IF–THEN statements to handle many different outcomes.

▼ The END IF keyword is used to mark the end of a multi-line IF–THEN statement, including multi-line statements with ELSEIF and ELSE clauses.

▼ The relational operators, equals (=), does not equal (<>), less than (<), greater than (>), less than or equal (<=), and greater than or equal (>=), enable programs to compare data in various ways.

▼ Logical operators (AND, OR, and NOT) enable an IF–THEN statement to evaluate more than one expression, yet they still resolve the expressions to a single true or false.

In the next chapter, you learn about looping constructs, which allow your programs to perform repetitive tasks—another thing that computers are extraordinarily good at.

CHAPTER 7

Repetitive Operations

(Over and Over and Over and. . .)

IN A NUTSHELL

▼ Understanding program looping

▼ Using FOR—NEXT, WHILE, and DO loops

▼ Knowing when to use each type of loop

A computer handles repetitive operations especially well—it never gets bored, and it can perform a task as well the 10,000th time as it did the first time. Consider, for example, a disk file containing 10,000 names and addresses. If you tried to type labels for all those people, you'd be seeing spots before your eyes in no time. A computer, on the other hand, can spit out all 10,000 labels tirelessly—and with nary a complaint to the union.

Every language must have some form of looping command to instruct a computer to perform repetitive tasks. QBasic features three types of looping: FOR–NEXT loops, WHILE loops, and DO loops. In this chapter, you learn to use these powerful programming techniques.

BUZZWORD

Looping
In computer programs, *looping* is the process of executing a block of statements repeatedly. Starting at the top of the block, the statements are executed until the program reaches the end of the block, at which point the program goes back to the top and starts over. The statements in the block may be repeated any number of times, from once to forever.

The *FOR-NEXT* Loop

(Around and around we go)

Probably the most often used loop in QBasic is the FOR–NEXT loop, which instructs a program to perform a block of code a specified number of times. You could, for example, use a FOR–NEXT loop to instruct your computer to print those 10,000 address labels. Because you don't currently have an address file, however, let's say you want to print your name on the screen six times. Listing 7.1 shows one way to do this.

Listing 7.1 REPEAT.BAS prints your name six times

```
CLS
INPUT "Please enter your name: ", name$
PRINT
PRINT name$
PRINT name$
PRINT name$
PRINT name$
PRINT name$
PRINT name$
```

Anywhere you have repeated commands may be a good place for a loop

IN SIMPLE TERMS

After clearing the screen, Listing 7.1 uses an INPUT statement to request the user's name. A series of PRINT statements then prints the name on-screen six times.

The program output for Listing 7.1 looks like this:

```
Please enter your name: Shawn

Shawn
Shawn
Shawn
Shawn
Shawn
Shawn
```

Look at Listing 7.1. See all those PRINT statements? As a computer programmer, whenever you see program code containing many identical instructions, a little bell should go off in your head. When you hear this little bell, you should do one of two things:

1. Answer your phone.

2. Say to yourself, "Hmmmm. This looks like a good place for a loop."

QBASIC FOR ROOKIES

Having many lines in your program containing identical instructions makes your program longer than necessary and wastes valuable memory. It also shows poor programming style. Unless you want your programming friends to snicker behind your back, learn to replace redundant program code with program loops.

TIP

In order to produce programs that are tightly written, shorter, and faster, always try to replace repetitive program code with program loops.

Listing 7.1 can be streamlined easily by using a FOR–NEXT loop, and Listing 7.2 shows how. The output of the second version is identical to the first (except a different name was entered); now the program is shorter and contains no redundant code.

Listing 7.2 LOOP1.BAS prints your name six times using a FOR–NEXT loop

Repeated commands replaced by a **FOR–NEXT** loop

```
CLS
INPUT "Please enter your name: ", name$
PRINT
FOR x = 1 TO 6
   PRINT name$
NEXT x
```

IN SIMPLE TERMS

After clearing the screen, Listing 7.1 requests the user's name with an INPUT statement. The user's name is then printed on the screen six times by a FOR–NEXT loop.

The output for Listing 7.2 looks like this:

```
Please enter your name: Justin

Justin
Justin
Justin
Justin
Justin
Justin
```

Look at the program line beginning with the keyword FOR. The loop starts with this line. The word FOR tells QBasic that you're starting a FOR–NEXT loop. After the word FOR is the *loop-control variable* x. The loop-control variable, which can have any legal numerical-variable name, is where QBasic stores the current loop count. See the number after the equal sign? QBasic uses this number to begin the loop count.

PLAY BALL!

BUZZWORD

Loop-Control Variable

A *loop-control variable* holds the current loop count. When the value of this variable reaches the requested loop count, the loop ends.

In Listing 7.2, when the FOR loop begins, QBasic places the number 1 in the variable x. The program then drops down to the next line, which prints the user's name. The line NEXT x tells QBasic to increment (increase by one) the loop-control variable and start again at the top of the loop. So, x becomes 2, and the program returns to the FOR line. The program then compares the value in x with the number following the keyword TO. If the loop count (in x) is less than or equal to the number following TO, the program executes the loop again. This process continues until x is greater than 6.

Whew! Got all that? Or did you fall asleep halfway through? If you just woke up, rub the fuzzies from your eyes and read the previous paragraph a couple of times to make sure it sinks in. If you still can't stay awake, take a nap.

PLAY BALL!

BUZZWORD

> ### Increment and Decrement
>
> In computer programs, variables are often incremented and decremented. When you *increment* a variable, you add some value to it. When you *decrement* a variable, you subtract some value from it. If the value of the increment or decrement is not explicit, it's assumed that the value is 1. For example, the statement "The program increments the variable num by 5" means that num is increased in value by 5. On the other hand, the statement "The program increments num" usually means that num is increased by 1.

Suppose you want to modify Listing 7.2 to print your name 10 times. What would you change? If you answered, "I'd change the 6 in the FOR line to 10," you win the Programmer of the Week award. If you answered, "I'd change my socks," you must go directly to jail. Do not pass Go, do not collect $200.

Adding the *STEP* clause

(Watch your step on this ride)

The previous example of a FOR–NEXT loop increments the loop counter by 1. But suppose you want a FOR–NEXT loop that counts from 5 to 50 by fives? You can do this by adding a STEP clause to your FOR–NEXT loop, as shown in Listing 7.3.

Listing 7.3 LOOP2.BAS uses the *STEP* clause in a *FOR* loop

```
CLS
INPUT "Please enter your name: ", name$
PRINT
FOR x = 5 TO 50 STEP 5
   PRINT name$
   PRINT "Loop counter value: ", x
NEXT x
```

This loop counts by fives

IN SIMPLE TERMS

After clearing the screen, Listing 7.3 uses an INPUT statement to get the user's name. The program then executes a FOR–NEXT loop that prints the user's name and the current value of the loop-control variable 10 times. Because the FOR–NEXT loop contains the clause STEP 5, 5 is added to the control variable (instead of the default, 1) each time through the loop.

Fig. 1 shows the output for Listing 7.3.

Fig. 1

```
Please enter your name: Stephen

Stephen
Loop counter value:          5
Stephen
Loop counter value:          10
Stephen
Loop counter value:          15
Stephen
Loop counter value:          20
Stephen
Loop counter value:          25
Stephen
Loop counter value:          30
Stephen
Loop counter value:          35
Stephen
Loop counter value:          40
Stephen
Loop counter value:          45
Stephen
Loop counter value:          50


Press any key to continue
```

When you run this program, you're asked to enter your name. The program then prints both your name and the current value of the loop variable 10 times. Besides showing how to use the STEP clause, this program also shows how you can place more than one command in the body of a FOR–NEXT loop. You can, in fact, have as many statements as you like between the FOR and NEXT.

BUZZWORD

> ### Body of a Loop
>
> The *body of a loop* comprises the commands that are performed each time through the loop. In a FOR–NEXT loop, for example, these are the statements between the FOR line and the NEXT line.

Look closely at the FOR–NEXT loop in Listing 7.3. Unlike the previous programs, this loop doesn't start counting at 1. Rather, the loop variable begins with a value of 5. Then, thanks to the STEP 5 clause, the loop variable is incremented by 5 each time through the loop. x goes from 5 to 10, from 10 to 15, and so on up to 50, resulting in ten loops.

Listing 7.4 shows how you can use the STEP clause to count backward. (Well, the STEP clause won't help *you* count backward, but it'll help your computer.) Notice that the loop limits are in reverse order; that is, the higher value comes first. Notice also that the STEP clause uses a negative value, which causes the loop count to be decremented (decreased) rather than incremented. Finally, notice that, no matter how hard you try, you can't whistle "The Star Spangled Banner" out of your right ear. This has little to do with computing, but is, nevertheless, one of the great mysteries of the cosmos.

Listing 7.4 LOOP3.BAS uses the *STEP* clause in a *FOR* loop to count backward

This loop counts backward by fives —

```
CLS
INPUT "Please enter your name: ", name$
PRINT
FOR x = 50 TO 5 STEP -5
   PRINT name$
   PRINT "Loop counter value: ", x
NEXT x
```

IN SIMPLE TERMS

After clearing the screen, Listing 7.4 uses an INPUT statement to get the user's name. The program then executes a FOR statement, which prints the user's name and the current value of the loop variable 10 times. Because the FOR loop contains the clause STEP -5, 5 is subtracted from the control variable each time through the loop.

The output for Listing 7.4 is shown in Fig. 2.

Fig. 2

```
Please enter your name: Christopher

Christopher
Loop counter value:          50
Christopher
Loop counter value:          45
Christopher
Loop counter value:          40
Christopher
Loop counter value:          35
Christopher
Loop counter value:          30
Christopher
Loop counter value:          25
Christopher
Loop counter value:          20
Christopher
Loop counter value:          15
Christopher
Loop counter value:          10
Christopher
Loop counter value:          5


Press any key to continue
```

QBASIC FOR ROOKIES

Using Variables in Loops

(Where we'll stop, nobody knows)

Just as with most numerical values in a program, you can substitute variables for the constants in a FOR–NEXT loop. In fact, you'll probably use variables in your loop limits as often as you use constants, if not more. Listing 7.5 shows how to do this and Fig. 3 shows the program's output.

Listing 7.5 LOOP4.BAS uses a variable for one of the loop limits

```
CLS
INPUT "Please enter your name: ", name$
INPUT "Please enter the print count: ", count
PRINT
FOR x = 1 TO count
  PRINT name$
  PRINT "Loop counter value: ", x
NEXT x
```

Using a variable makes this loop more versatile

IN SIMPLE TERMS

After clearing the screen, Listing 7.5 uses two INPUT statements to get the user's name and the number of times the user would like his name printed. The program then prints a blank line, after which it executes a FOR–NEXT loop that prints the user's name and the current value of the loop-control variable count times.

Fig.
3

```
Please enter your name: Lynn
Please enter the print count: 10

Lynn
Loop counter value:        1
Lynn
Loop counter value:        2
Lynn
Loop counter value:        3
Lynn
Loop counter value:        4
Lynn
Loop counter value:        5
Lynn
Loop counter value:        6
Lynn
Loop counter value:        7
Lynn
Loop counter value:        8
Lynn
Loop counter value:        9
Lynn
Loop counter value:        10

Press any key to continue
```

When you run this program, you're asked to enter your name and the number of times you want it printed. The program then prints your name the requested number of times. As you can see in Listing 7.5, you can have the program print your name any number of times because the loop's upper limit is contained in the variable count; count gets its value from you at the start of each program run.

Using variables in FOR–NEXT loops makes your programs more flexible and produces a powerful programming construct. As you'll soon see, you can use variables with other types of loops, too. In fact, you can use a numerical variable in a program in most places a numerical value is required. You can even use numerical variables in salads, but they taste bitter and leave a yucky film on your tongue.

QBASIC FOR ROOKIES

Using *WHILE* Loops

(Getting dizzy yet?)

Another type of loop you can use in your programs is the WHILE loop. Unlike a FOR–NEXT loop, which loops the number of times given in the loop limits, a WHILE loop continues executing until its control expression becomes true. The *control expression* is a Boolean expression much like the Boolean expressions you used with IF statements. In other words, any expression that evaluates to true or false can be used as a control expression for a WHILE loop. Listing 7.6 shows a WHILE loop in action and Fig. 4 shows the program's output.

Listing 7.6 LOOP5.BAS demonstrates a WHILE loop

You must initialize a ——— WHILE loop's control variable

```
CLS
num = 1
WHILE num <> 0
    INPUT "Please enter a number: ", num
WEND
PRINT
PRINT "Looping is finished."
```

IN SIMPLE TERMS

After clearing the screen, Listing 7.6 sets the variable num to 1, which allows the program to enter the WHILE loop. The WHILE loop contains an INPUT statement that asks the user to enter a number. The loop repeats until the user enters a 0, after which the program prints a brief message and ends.

Fig. 4

```
Please enter a number: 2
Please enter a number: 6
Please enter a number: 45
Please enter a number: 3
Please enter a number: -5
Please enter a number: 7
Please enter a number: 8

Looping is finished.




Press any key to continue
```

PLAY BALL!

BUZZWORD

Loop-Control Expression

A *loop-control expression* is a Boolean expression that determines whether a loop should continue or end. In a WHILE loop, when the control expression becomes false, the loop ends. As long as the control expression is true, the loop continues.

How does the WHILE loop in Listing 7.6 work? First, the loop variable num is set to 1. Then, at the start of the WHILE loop, the program compares the value in num with the constant 0. If these two values don't match, the expression evaluates to false, and the program executes the body of the loop, which in this case is a single INPUT statement. This statement gets a number from the user and stores it in the variable num. The program then comes to the WEND keyword (it stands for *WHILE END*), which tells QBasic that it has reached the end of the loop and must now go back and check the value of num again.

If the user entered a value other than 0, the two values in the loop's control expression again don't match, and the INPUT statement executes again. If the values do match, the control expression evaluates to true, the loop ends, and the program branches to the first statement after the WEND, which, in the case of Listing 7.6, is a PRINT statement.

Notice how the program sets the variable num to 1 before the WHILE loop starts. This is important, since it ensures that the value in num starts at a value other than 0. If num did happen to start at 0, the program would never get to the INPUT statement within the WHILE loop. Instead, the loop's control expression would immediately evaluate to true, and the program would branch to the PRINT statement. Mistakes like this make programmers growl at their loved ones and answer the phone with, "What do you want, butthead?"

BUZZWORD

Initializing

Initializing a variable means setting it to its starting value. In QBasic, all numeric variables are automatically initialized to 0. If you need a variable to start at a different value, you must initialize it yourself. Warning: Always initialize any variable used in a WHILE loop's control expression. Failure to do so may result in your program skipping over the loop entirely.

The DO Loop

(Nearing the end of the ride)

QBasic also features DO loops. A DO loop is much like a WHILE loop, except a DO loop evaluates its control expression at the end of the loop rather than at the beginning. So the body of the loop—the statements between

the beginning and end of the loop—is always executed at least once. In a WHILE loop, the body of the loop may or may not ever get executed. Listing 7.7 shows how a DO loop works and Fig. 5 displays the program's output.

Listing 7.7 LOOP6.BAS demonstrates a DO loop

A **DO** loop checks its control expression at the bottom of the loop ———

```
CLS
DO
    INPUT "Please enter a number: ", num
LOOP UNTIL num = 0
PRINT
PRINT "Looping is finished."
```

IN SIMPLE TERMS

After clearing the screen, Listing 7.7 enters a DO loop. In the loop, the user is asked to enter a number. The INPUT statement that requests the number repeats until the user enters a value of O, after which the program prints a brief message and ends.

Fig. 5

```
Please enter a number: 4
Please enter a number: 3
Please enter a number: 6
Please enter a number: 7
Please enter a number: 2345
Please enter a number: -756
Please enter a number: 4.576
Please enter a number: 0

Looping is finished.




Press any key to continue
```

QBASIC FOR ROOKIES

When you run Listing 7.7, you're asked to enter a number. As long as you enter a number other than 0, the program continues to loop. When you finally enter 0, the loop ends.

Notice that you don't need to initialize the loop-control variable num before entering the loop. num gets its value from the INPUT statement that comes before the loop's control statement is executed. So if people have stopped calling your house because they're tired of being called buttheads, try changing your WHILE loops to DO loops. The variable num always holds a valid value when the program reaches the LOOP UNTIL portion of the loop, where num is compared with 0.

The DO loop actually has two forms, one that ends with LOOP UNTIL and one that ends with LOOP WHILE. LOOP UNTIL allows a loop to continue until the control expression becomes true. LOOP WHILE allows a loop to continue until the control expression becomes false. For example, in Listing 7.7, the loop continues until num equals 0. You could reverse this logic by using a LOOP WHILE, rather than a LOOP UNTIL. In this case, the last line of the loop would read LOOP WHILE num <> 0, which forces the loop to continue as long as num doesn't equal 0.

TIP

Different looping methods work best in different programming situations. Although experience is the best teacher, you should keep some things in mind when selecting a looping construct. When you want a loop to run a specific number of times, the FOR—NEXT loop is usually the best choice. When you want a loop to run until a certain condition is met, the WHILE or DO loop works best. Remember that the body of a DO loop is always executed at least once, because the control expression is checked at the bottom of the loop. A WHILE loop, on the

other hand, is not guaranteed to execute at all, because its control expression is evaluated first, at the top of the loop. Table 7.1 summarizes when to use the different types of loops.

Table 7.1. Loop requirements versus loop type

Circumstance	Best method
1. Loop a specific number of times	FOR–NEXT
2. Loop until a condition is met	WHILE or DO
3. Loop 0 or more times	WHILE
4. Loop at least once	DO

Putting It Together

(One last spin)

You've learned a lot about program looping in this chapter, and you're probably not sure how or why you would use these techniques. Listings 7.8 through 7.10 give you the chance to broaden your experience with the three looping constructs. When you run any of the programs, you're asked to enter a string that contains the word loop. After you enter the string, the program uses one of the looping techniques to find and mark the location of the substring loop in the string you entered.

QBASIC FOR ROOKIES

All three programs yield similar program output (Fig. 6), but each uses a different looping technique to get the job done. Be sure you understand these programs before you move on to the next chapter. Looping is a valuable tool to use when writing programs. You'll use it more than a cat uses a litter box.

Listing 7.8 LOOPDEM1.BAS uses a FOR–NEXT loop to locate a substring (a part of a larger string)

```
CLS
INPUT "Enter a string containing the word 'loop': ", s$
PRINT

location = 0
FOR x = 1 TO LEN(s$)
    IF MID$(s$, x, 4) = "loop" THEN location = x
NEXT x

IF location = 0 THEN
    PRINT "Word 'loop' not found."
ELSE
    PRINT s$
    FOR x = 1 TO location - 1
        PRINT " ";
    NEXT x
    PRINT "^"
END IF
```

This loop finds the substring **loop**

This loop sets the printing position of the caret

IN SIMPLE TERMS

After clearing the screen, Listing 7.8 asks the user to enter a string containing the word loop. It then initializes the variable location, which holds the location of the substring loop to 0. A FOR–NEXT loop is then executed. This loop's limit is from 1 to the length of the string that the user entered.

Within the loop, the string function MID$ uses the loop-control variable x as the starting location at which to check for the requested substring. By using this variable, MID$ starts its string comparisons at the first character and moves forward through the string a character at a time looking for the substring loop. When the IF statement evaluates to true (when MID$ finds the substring), the variable location is set to the value of the loop variable x. The FOR–NEXT loop continues until it reaches the end of the string.

(If you've forgotten how string functions such as MID$ work, please review Chapter 5.)

If location is still 0 when the loop finishes, the substring was not found. The program then prints an error message. If location is greater than 0, the program prints the contents of s$, which is the string the user entered. The program then uses another FOR–NEXT loop to print enough spaces to place the cursor immediately beneath the first character of the substring loop, at which point it prints a caret marking the substring's location.

Listing 7.9 LOOPDEM2.BAS uses a WHILE loop to locate a substring

```
CLS
INPUT "Enter a string containing the word 'loop': ", s$
PRINT

x = 1
WHILE (MID$(s$, x, 4) <> "loop") AND (x < LEN(s$))
  x = x + 1
WEND
```

*Now you're doing the same thing with a **WHILE** loop*

continues

165

QBASIC FOR ROOKIES

Listing 7.9 Continued

```
IF x = LEN(s$) THEN
  PRINT "Word 'loop' not found."
ELSE
  PRINT s$
  FOR i = 1 TO x - 1
    PRINT " ";
  NEXT i
  PRINT "^"
END IF
```

IN SIMPLE TERMS

Listing 7.9 works much like Listing 7.8, except this version of the program uses a WHILE loop to locate the substring. After the user enters a string, the loop counter x is initialized to 1 to ensure that the program gets into the WHILE loop. The loop's control expression uses the logical operator AND to make two comparisons. In the first comparison, MID$ checks for the substring. The second comparison ensures that the loop won't continue beyond the length of the string, which would happen if the user's string did not contain the word loop. When the WHILE loop ends, the variable x contains the location of the substring if the string was found or the length of s$ if the substring wasn't found. The results of the search are printed using similar code to that found in Listing 7.8.

Listing 7.10 LOOPDEM3.BAS uses a *DO* loop to locate a substring

```
CLS
INPUT "Enter a string containing the word 'loop': ", s$
PRINT

x = 0
DO
   x = x + 1
LOOP UNTIL (MID$(s$, x, 4) = "loop") OR (x = LEN(s$))

IF x = LEN(s$) THEN
   PRINT "Word 'loop' not found."
ELSE
   PRINT s$
   FOR i = 1 TO x - 1
     PRINT " ";
   NEXT i
   PRINT "^"
END IF
```

And now you're using a **DO** loop to find the substring

IN SIMPLE TERMS

Listing 7.10 works much like Listing 7.9, except that it uses a DO loop rather than a WHILE loop to search through the user's string. In this version of the program, the loop continues until the substring is found or until the loop counter x is equal to the length of the string the user entered. In the latter case, the substring is not in the string, so an error message is printed. Otherwise, the user's string is displayed and the location of the substring is marked.

QBASIC FOR ROOKIES

Fig.
6

```
Enter a string containing the word 'loop': jfhyrhgf loophfgyriie
jfhyrhgf loophfgyriie
             ^




Press any key to continue
```

Common Rookie Mistakes

Using the wrong type of loop. As mentioned previously, each type of looping construct works best in different circumstances. For example, a FOR–NEXT loop should be used only for loops that always execute from the starting limit to the ending limit. If you find yourself needing to get out of a FOR–NEXT loop before the loop has run its course, you should probably be using a WHILE loop or DO loop.

Changing the value of a loop-control variable within the loop. The value of a FOR–NEXT loop's loop-control variable should never be changed directly by your code. Except in rare circumstances, FOR–NEXT loops should always be allowed to run their full cycle. If a loop is not working the way you expect it to, make sure you're not accidentally changing a loop-control variable in your code.

Faulty logic in a control expression. Just like the expressions used in IF statements, the control expressions used in WHILE and DO loops can be built using the logical operators AND, OR, and NOT. However, the more

complex a control expression becomes, the more likely it is that the expression doesn't mean what you think it means. Try to keep loop-control expressions as simple as possible, and study them carefully to be sure they represent the logic you want. (You can see examples of using logical operators in loop-control expressions in Listings 7.9 and 7.10.)

Forgetting to initialize a loop-control variable in a WHILE *loop.* Remember that a WHILE loop will execute only if the control expression evaluates to true. In other words, a WHILE loop's control expression should almost always evaluate to false the first time through the loop. The only exception is when the WHILE loop is designed not to execute under certain circumstances.

Infinite loops. New programmers are infamous for creating WHILE and DO loops that never end. For example, if you write a WHILE loop whose control expression can never become true, your loop will loop forever. When this happens, it looks to you as though your program has "locked up" your machine (your computer has stopped dead in its tracks and will accept no input). But your program actually is looping frantically, with no hope of ever moving on. The only way out of this predicament is to press Ctrl-Break to terminate the program. If pressing Ctrl-Break shows that your program was in the middle of a WHILE or DO loop when it got hung up, it's time to check the loop's control expression for conditions that cannot possibly be met.

Summing Up

▼ Repetitive operations in a computer program can be handled efficiently by program loops, including FOR–NEXT loops, WHILE loops, and DO loops.

▼ A FOR–NEXT loop instructs a program to execute a block of commands a given number of times. In the FOR–NEXT loop

```
FOR x = num1 TO num2: NEXT x
```

the variable x is the loop's control variable. The loop limits are the values of num1 and num2.

▼ By adding a STEP clause to a FOR–NEXT loop, you can make the loop-control variable count up or down in any increment or decrement. For example, the loop

```
FOR x = 20 to 10 STEP -2: NEXT x
```

counts backward by twos, from 20 to 10.

▼ You can use a numeric variable for either of the two loop limits in a FOR–NEXT loop.

▼ A WHILE loop repeats until its loop-control expression evaluates to true. The control expression can be any Boolean expression (one that evaluates to true or false). These are the same kinds of expressions you used with IF statements.

▼ A DO loop always executes at least once, because its control expression is at the bottom of the loop rather than at the top.

▼ The DO loop has two forms. In the first form—the DO/UNTIL loop—the loop continues until the control expression becomes true. In the second form—the DO/WHILE loop—the loop continues until the control expression becomes false.

If you're still a little fuzzy about how to use program loops, don't worry. As with most programming concepts, practice leads to understanding. For now, though, it's time to learn how to store many values under a single variable name. These special variables, called arrays, are the subject of the next chapter.

CHAPTER 8
Powerful Structures
(Building a Better Beast)

IN A NUTSHELL

▼ Learning about arrays

▼ Using arrays with loops

▼ Understanding numerical and string arrays

▼ Using DATA and READ to initialize arrays

As you've learned by now, using variables makes your programs flexible. Thanks to variables, you can conveniently store data in your programs and retrieve it by name. You can also get input from your program's user. The best thing about variables is that they can constantly change value. They're called variables, after all, because they're variable!

Until now, you've learned about various types of numerical variables, including integers, long integers, single-precision variables, and double-precision variables. You also know about string variables, which can hold text. Now that you have a good understanding of these data types, it's time to explore one last data type, a handy data structure called an array.

An Introduction to Arrays

(A clever solution to a tricky problem)

Often in your programs, you'll want to store many values that are related in some way. Suppose you manage a bowling league and you want to keep track of each player's average. One way to do this is to give each player a variable in your program, as shown in Listing 8.1.

> **Listing 8.1 BOWLING1.BAS stores bowling averages for four bowlers**

```
CLS
INPUT "Enter Fred's average: ", avg1
INPUT "Enter Mary's average: ", avg2
INPUT "Enter Thomas's average: ", avg3
INPUT "Enter Alice's average: ", avg4
PRINT
PRINT "BOWLERS' AVERAGES"
PRINT "----------------"
```

Four different variables are required to store the bowlers' averages

```
PRINT "Fred:"; avg1
PRINT "Mary:"; avg2
PRINT "Thomas:"; avg3
PRINT "Alice:"; avg4
```

IN SIMPLE TERMS

Listing 8.1 uses four INPUT statements to get bowling averages for four bowlers. These averages are stored in the variables avg1, avg2, avg3, and avg4. After the user inputs the averages, the program displays them along with each bowler's name.

When you run Listing 8.1, you're asked to enter bowling averages for each of four bowlers. After you enter these averages, they're displayed on-screen as follows:

```
Enter Fred's average: 140
Enter Mary's average: 154
Enter Thomas's average: 207
Enter Alice's average: 125

BOWLERS' AVERAGES
- - - - - - - - - - - - - - - -
Fred: 140
Mary: 154
Thomas: 207
Alice: 125
```

Nothing too tricky going on here, right?

Now examine the listing. Remember in the last chapter when you learned to keep an eye out for repetitive program code? How about all those INPUT statements in Listing 8.1? The only real difference between

them is the name of the variable used to store the input value. If you could find some way to make a loop out of this code, you'd need only one INPUT line to input all the data and only one PRINT line to display the averages for all four bowlers. You could, in fact, use a FOR–NEXT loop that counts from 1 to 4.

But how can you use a loop when you're stuck with four different variables? The answer is an array. An *array* is a variable that can hold more than one value. When you first studied variables, you learned that a variable is like a box in memory that holds a single value. Now, if you take a bunch of these boxes and put them together, what do you have? (No, the answer isn't "a bunch of variables smooshed together.") You'd have an array. For example, to store the bowling averages for your four bowlers, you'd need an array that can hold four values. You could call this array avg.

PLAY BALL!

BUZZWORD

Array

An *array* is a type of variable that can hold many values, rather than just one. It is actually a section of your computer's memory that contains enough room to store the number of values you specify.

Now you have an array called avg that can hold four bowling averages. But how can you retrieve each individual average from the array? You could run out on your front lawn in your skivvies, wave a plucked chicken over your head, and shout praises to the gods of computing. However, an easier way—and one that doesn't amuse the neighbors quite so much—is to add something called a subscript to the array's name.

A *subscript* is a number that identifies the box in which an array value is stored. For example, to refer to the first average in your avg array, you'd write avg(1). The subscript is the number in parentheses. In this case, you're referring to the first average in the array. To refer to the second average, you'd write avg(2). The third and fourth averages are avg(3) and avg(4). Get the idea?

PLAY BALL!

BUZZWORD

Subscript
A *subscript* is the number in parentheses after an array's name. The subscript identifies which value in the array you want to access. For example, in the array name numbers%(10), the subscript is 10, which refers to the tenth value stored in the array numbers%().

If you're a little confused, look at Fig. 1, which shows how the avg() array might look in memory. In this case, the four bowling averages are 145, 192, 160, and 203. The value of avg(1) is 145, the value of avg(2) is 192, the value of avg(3) is 160, and the value of avg(4) is 203.

Fig. 1

AVG%(1)	AVG%(2)	AVG%(3)	AVG%(4)
145	192	160	203

Using a Variable as a Subscript

(The old indirect approach)

As you've learned, most numerical constants in a QBasic program can be replaced by numerical variables. Suppose, then, you were to use the variable x as the subscript for the array avg(). Then (based on the averages in Fig. 1), if the value of x were 2, the value of avg(x) would be 192. If the value of x were 4, the value of avg(x) would be 203.

QBASIC FOR ROOKIES

Now take one last gigantic intuitive leap (c'mon, you can do it), and think about using your subscript variable x as both the control variable in a FOR–NEXT loop and the subscript for the avg() array. If you use a FOR–NEXT loop that counts from 1 to 4, you can use a single INPUT line to get all four players' averages. Listing 8.2 shows how this is done.

Listing 8.2 BOWLING2.BAS uses an array to store bowling averages for four bowlers

```
CLS
DIM avg%(4)

FOR x = 1 TO 4
  INPUT "Enter bowler's average: ", avg(%x)
NEXT x

PRINT
FOR x = 1 TO 4
  PRINT "Average for bowler"; x; ": "; avg(%x)
NEXT x
```

A single array can hold all the averages

IN SIMPLE TERMS

Listing 8.2 first clears the screen and then dimensions a four-element array. The first FOR–NEXT loop retrieves four averages from the user and stores them in the integer array avg%(). The second FOR–NEXT loop displays the averages.

Here is the output from Listing 8.2:

```
Enter bowler's average: 146
Enter bowler's average: 192
Enter bowler's average: 156
Enter bowler's average: 137
```

```
Average for bowler 1 :   146
Average for bowler 2 :   192
Average for bowler 3 :   156
Average for bowler 4 :   137
```

At the top of Listing 8.2, you'll see a strange new keyword, DIM. DIM is short for "dimension" and is used to tell QBasic how much room in memory you need for your array. In BOWLING2.BAS, you've "dimensioned" the array as avg%(4), which tells QBasic that you need to store four integers in this array.

CAUTION

When you dimension your arrays, make sure you have enough room for the data you need to store. Once you dimension an array, QBasic will not allow you to store or retrieve values beyond the end of the array. For example, if you dimension an array as numbers%(10) and then try to access numbers%(11), your program will come to a crashing halt and give you a subscript-out-of-range error. But don't make your arrays bigger than they need to be, because this wastes your computer's memory.

Do you understand how the program works? In the first FOR–NEXT loop, the variable x starts with a value of 1. The value retrieved by the INPUT statement is stored in avg%(x), which means that, when x equals 1, the value is stored in avg%(1). The next time through the loop, x equals 2, so the value retrieved by the INPUT statement is stored in avg%(2). This continues until x has incremented from 1 to 4 and becomes 5, and the FOR–NEXT loop ends. The second FOR–NEXT loop works similarly, incrementing x from 1 to 4 and printing the contents of the array one element at a time.

QBASIC FOR ROOKIES

PLAY BALL!

BUZZWORD

Elements

The little memory boxes that make up an array are called *elements* of the array. For example, in an array named `numbers%()`, `numbers%(1)` is the first element of the array, `numbers%(2)` is the second element, and so on.

CATCH THIS!

All arrays actually have what's called a zeroth element. That is, you can actually start storing data in element 0 of an array. This means that an array that's been dimensioned as `numbers%(2)` has three elements: `numbers%(0)`, `numbers%(1)`, and `numbers%(2)`. However, most QBasic programmers ignore the zeroth element of an array because it's confusing to think of element 0 as being the first element.

String Arrays

(Yet another fantabulous example of programming prowess)

Listing 8.2 shows how handy arrays can be, but there's something missing from the program. First, there's no built-in Space Invaders game, so using this program for long periods of time is not only *not* exciting but also downright boring. More to the point, though, the bowlers' names are missing. In this version of the program, you've resorted to using a bowler number rather than each bowler's name. You can get around this problem easily, by creating an array to hold strings. (You can get over the Space Invaders problem by taking a Nintendo break.) Listing 8.3 shows how this is done.

> ### Listing 8.3 BOWLING3.BAS uses an array for the bowlers' names and averages

```
CLS
DIM avg%(4), name$(4)

FOR x = 1 TO 4
  INPUT "Enter bowler's name: ", name$(x)
    INPUT "Enter bowler's average: ", avg%(x)
NEXT x

PRINT
PRINT "BOWLERS' AVERAGES"
PRINT "----------------"
FOR x = 1 TO 4
  PRINT "Average for "; name$(x); ": "; avg%(x)
NEXT x
```

A string array can hold all the bowlers' names ——

The subscript **x** accesses both arrays and thus matches the bowlers' names with their —— averages

IN SIMPLE TERMS

Listing 8.3 first clears the screen and then dimensions two four-element arrays, one for integers and one for strings. (Notice that you can dimension several arrays on one line by separating the array names with commas.) The first FOR—NEXT loop retrieves four names and averages from the user and stores them in the arrays name$() and avg%(). The second FOR—NEXT loop displays the names and averages.

The output for Listing 8.3 looks like this:

```
Enter bowler's name: Fred
Enter bowler's average: 156
Enter bowler's name: Mary
Enter bowler's average: 176
```

QBASIC FOR ROOKIES

```
Enter bowler's name: Thomas
Enter bowler's average: 135
Enter bowler's name: Alice
Enter bowler's average: 185

BOWLERS' AVERAGES
- - - - - - - - - - - - - - - - -
Average for Fred:    156
Average for Mary:    176
Average for Thomas:   135
Average for Alice:   185
```

When you run Listing 8.3, you're asked to enter not only the bowlers' averages but also their names. The names are stored in a string array, and the averages are stored in an integer array. Because both arrays used the same subscript value for each bowler's name and average, the first name in the string array matches the first average in the integer array, the second name matches the second average, and so on. It's then a simple matter to use another loop to print out the names and averages.

Initializing Arrays

(Starting off right)

Your bowling-averages program still isn't as efficient as it could be. Why, for example, should you have to enter the name of each bowler every time you run the program? Do you really need that much typing practice? In most cases, the names of the bowlers won't change. There must be some way to store data in your programs without having to enter it from the keyboard. You could get a grease pencil, write the bowlers' names on your computer's screen, and hope they sink in. But a better (and more dependable) method is to use QBasic's DATA and READ statements.

BUZZWORD

Data

Data is information that you manipulate or store in your program. When you want to place data into your program without having to manually enter it, you can use a DATA statement. For example, the statement DATA 1,5,65,10 makes the four integers 1, 5, 65, and 10 part of your program's data. This data is saved along with the rest of your program lines. Reading data means moving the data from one place to another, usually from a DATA statement and into a variable of some kind. To read data from a DATA statement, you use the READ command. For example, the statement READ x% reads the first value in a DATA statement into the variable x.

When you start a program line with the keyword DATA, QBasic knows that the values which follow DATA should be stored with the program. Then each time you run the program, that data is available for your use. To store the names of your bowlers, you'd use the following line:

```
DATA Fred,Mary,Thomas,Alice
```

Notice the commas between the names. This is how QBasic separates one piece of data from another.

Now that you have a way of storing your bowlers' names along with the program, how can you get those names into your string array? Easy! By using QBasic's READ command. To read the first name, you might write

```
READ name$(1)
```

This command takes the next value from the program's DATA statements and stuffs it into name$(1). In the DATA statement just shown, name$(1) becomes Fred. The data pointer, which always points to the next data item in the list, is then moved to Mary. The next READ statement then reads Mary, the data pointer is moved to Thomas, and so on. When all the data items have been read, the data list is empty—until the program runs again and the cycle is repeated. (By the way, data in your program can be placed in more than one DATA statement. In fact, you can have as many DATA statements as you like.)

Listing 8.4 shows how the DATA and READ statements work. It's important that you understand this program because this is the way arrays are often initialized.

> **Listing 8.4 BOWLING4.BAS stores bowlers' names in a DATA statement**

```
CLS
DIM avg%(4), name$(4)

FOR x = 1 TO 4
  READ name$(x)
    PRINT "What's "; name$(x); "'s average";
    INPUT avg%(x)
NEXT x

PRINT
PRINT "BOWLERS' AVERAGES"
PRINT "-----------------"
FOR x = 1 TO 4
  PRINT "Average for "; name$(x); ": "; avg%(x)
NEXT x

DATA Fred,Mary,Thomas,Alice
```

Data from the DATA statement is read here —— READ name$(x)

You can store all kinds of data in a DATA statement —— DATA Fred,Mary,Thomas,Alice

IN SIMPLE TERMS

After clearing the screen, Listing 8.4 dimensions two four-element arrays, one for integers and one for strings. Then a FOR–NEXT loop counts from 1 to 4, reading bowlers' names from the DATA statement and requesting the bowlers' averages from the user. The bowlers' names are stored in the string array name$(), and the bowlers' averages are stored in the integer array avg%(). The second FOR–NEXT loop displays the names and averages.

Listing 8.4 produces the following output:

```
What's Fred's average? 165
What's Mary's average? 134
What's Thomas's average? 187
What's Alice's average? 174

BOWLERS' AVERAGES
- - - - - - - - - - - - - - - -
Average for Fred:   165
Average for Mary:   134
Average for Thomas:   187
Average for Alice:   174
```

TIP

You don't have to use DATA and READ statements to initialize arrays. You can also initialize arrays by using assignment statements, just as with regular variables. For example, the line

```
FOR x = 1 to 10: num%(x) = 0: NEXT x
```

initializes to 0 every element of the array num%() (assuming, of course, that the array was dimensioned as num%(10)).

183

QBASIC FOR ROOKIES

When you run Listing 8.4, you're no longer asked to enter each bowler's name. Instead, the names are read by the program, using the data following the DATA statement. Each time through the first FOR–NEXT loop, a bowler's name is read from the data, and you're asked to provide that bowler's average. By the end of the loop, all four bowlers' names and averages have been placed in their respective arrays.

TIP

It doesn't matter where in your program you place your DATA statements. QBasic always starts reading from the DATA statement closest to the top of the program, wherever it happens to be. However, many programmers place their DATA statements at the end of their programs in order to keep them out of the way.

You can use DATA and READ statements with any kind of data. You can even mix different types of data on a single DATA line. You just have to be sure that you read each data item into the right variable type. You couldn't, for example, read a string into a numerical variable. To see how this works, suppose that you now want to include each bowler's average and name in the program's data. Listing 8.5 is the bowling-averages program with this change installed.

Listing 8.5 BOWLING5.BAS stores the bowlers' names and averages in a DATA statement

```
CLS
DIM avg%(4), name$(4)

FOR x = 1 TO 4
    READ name$(x) ─────────────── A string is read from the
    READ avg%(x) ─────────────── DATA statement
NEXT x                             Then an integer is read
```

```
PRINT
PRINT "BOWLERS' AVERAGES"
PRINT "----------------"
FOR x = 1 TO 4
   PRINT "Average for "; name$(x); ":"; avg%(x)
NEXT x

DATA Fred,145,Mary,192,Thomas,160,Alice,203
```

*The strings and integers are stored in the **DATA** statement in the order in which they will be read* ────

IN SIMPLE TERMS

After clearing the screen, Listing 8.5 dimensions two four-element arrays, one for integers and one for strings. Then a FOR–NEXT loop counts from 1 to 4, reading bowlers' names and averages from the DATA statement. The bowlers' names are stored in the string array name$(), and the bowlers' averages are stored in the integer array avg%(). The second FOR–NEXT loop displays the names and averages.

Here is the output for Listing 8.5:

```
BOWLERS' AVERAGES
----------------
Average for Fred: 145
Average for Mary: 192
Average for Thomas: 160
Average for Alice: 203
```

Listing 8.5 is almost the same program as Listing 8.4. The main difference is that you no longer have to enter data from the keyboard. All the data is contained in the program's DATA statement. If a bowler's average changes, you need to change only the appropriate entry in the DATA statement.

Common Rookie Mistakes

Allowing array subscripts to go out of bounds. It's easier than you might think—especially when you use WHILE or DO loops—to allow an array's subscript to get larger (or smaller) than the array can handle. Once you've dimensioned an array, you can never access an array element beyond the end of the array. If you do, your program will crash (come to an abrupt halt). If you run into a program that gives you subscript-out-of-bounds errors, first check subscript variables used within loops.

Reading data into the wrong type of variable. The DATA and READ statements provide a handy and powerful way to store and retrieve data from within your programs. However, you must be careful—especially when using mixed data types in a DATA statement—that every READ's variable matches the type of data that will be read. If your READ statements generate syntax errors during the program's run, you've probably got mismatched data types.

Summing Up

▼ Arrays allow you to store many values under a single variable name.

▼ An array's subscript, which is a number within parentheses appended to the array's name, identifies each element of the array.

▼ By using a numerical variable for an array's subscript, you can easily access each element of the array within a loop.

▼ To tell QBasic how large an array should be, you must dimension the array by using a DIM statement.

▼ QBasic's DATA statement allows you to store various types of data within your programs. The READ statement reads data from a DATA statement and places it in the appropriate variables.

You now know most of the basics of programming in QBasic—everything you need to know to produce useful and powerful programs. But before you go on your way, you need to learn about modular programming and program debugging. These important topics are covered in the final chapter.

CHAPTER 9

Breaking Things Down

(Tying Up Some Loose Ends)

IN A NUTSHELL

▼ Writing modular programs
▼ Designing programs from the top down
▼ Writing subroutines and functions
▼ Using QBasic's debugger

Until now, your programs have been pretty short, each designed to demonstrate a single programming technique. When you start writing real programs, however, you'll quickly discover that they can grow to many pages of code. When programs get long, they also get harder to organize and read. To overcome this problem, professional programmers developed something called modular programming, which you study in this chapter.

Another problem you'll have when writing full-length programs is finding and fixing programming errors. When a program is only a few lines long, you can easily examine each line of code and locate problems. But when a program grows to hundreds or even thousands of lines, you won't want to look at every line in the program (unless you're the type of person who likes to read phone books from cover to cover). Instead, you'll want to isolate the problem to a specific part of the program so you can find your error more quickly. QBasic's built-in debugger, which you also study in this chapter, can help you find these errors.

The Top-Down Approach to Programming

(A programmer's pyramid plan)

Like I said, long programs are hard to organize and read. A full-length program might contain 10 or more pages of code, and trying to find a specific part of the program in all that code can be tough. To solve this problem, you can use modular programming techniques. Using these techniques, you can break a long program into individual modules, with each module performing a specific task.

To understand how modular programming works, consider how you might organize the cleaning of a house. (The only reasonable way to clean my house is to douse it with gasoline and throw in a lighted

match, but we won't get into that just now.) The main task might be called CLEAN HOUSE. Thinking about cleaning an entire house, however, can be overwhelming—especially my house. So, to make the task easier, you can break it down into a number of smaller steps. These steps might be CLEAN LIVING ROOM, CLEAN BEDROOM, CLEAN KITCHEN, and CLEAN BATHROOM.

After breaking the housecleaning task down into room-by-room steps, you have a better idea of what to do. But cleaning a room is also a pretty big task—especially if it hasn't been done in a while or if you have cats coughing up fur balls all over the place. So why not break each room into steps, too? For example, cleaning the living room could be broken down into PICK UP ROOM, DUST AND POLISH, CLEAN FURNI-TURE, and VACUUM RUG. After breaking each room's cleaning down into steps, your housecleaning job is organized much like a pyramid, with the general task on top. As you work your way down the pyramid, from the main task, to the room-by-room list, and finally to the tasks for each room, the tasks get more and more specific.

Of course, when you clean your house, you usually don't write a list of steps. If you're an efficient housecleaner, the steps are organized in your mind. (If you clean house like me, there are only two steps: TURN ON TV and COLLAPSE ON COUCH.) However, when you write a program, which is a more conceptual task, you may not have a clear idea of exactly what must be done. Consequently, you may become overwhelmed by the project. Overwhelmed programmers are easy to spot. They stare at their computer screens blankly and often break into bouts of weeping.

Breaking programming tasks down into steps, or modules, is called modular programming. And when you break your program's modules down into even smaller modules—as we did with the task of cleaning a house—you're using a top-down approach to program design. By using top-down programming techniques, you can write any program as a series of small, easy-to-handle tasks.

QBasic provides two types of modules that you can use when you write programs. The first type, subroutines, is covered in the next section. The second type of module, functions, is covered later in this chapter.

Using Subroutines

(Blocks in the pyramid)

One type of program module is a subroutine. A *subroutine* is like a small program within your main program. If you were writing a house-cleaning program, the subroutines in the main module might be called `CleanLivingRoom`, `CleanBedroom`, `CleanKitchen`, and `CleanBathroom`. The `CleanLivingRoom` subroutine would contain all the steps needed to clean the living room, the `CleanBedroom` subroutine would contain all the steps needed to clean a bedroom, and so on.

Of course, it takes an extremely talented programmer to get a computer to clean a house. (If you manage that trick, contact me immediately.) We need a more computer-oriented example. Suppose you want to write a program that draws a moving arrow on-screen. (Don't ask why.) Listing 9.1 shows how to do this.

Listing 9.1 SUBRTN1.BAS shoots an arrow across your screen

```
                    CLS
                    FOR x% = 1 TO 70
Subroutine ──────── CALL Arrow(x%)
call                NEXT x%

                    SUB Arrow (x%)
Next line to ────── LOCATE 5, x%
execute after         PRINT ">>--->"
subroutine            FOR delay = 1 TO 100: NEXT delay
call
```

```
     LOCATE 5, x%
     IF x% < 70 THEN PRINT "        "
END SUB
```

IN SIMPLE TERMS

Listing 9.1 first clears the screen, then calls the subroutine Arrow 70 times within a FOR—NEXT loop. The Arrow subroutine draws the arrow on-screen at the position stored in x%, which is the value of the FOR—NEXT loop's control variable. By constantly changing the position of the arrow, it appears to fly across the screen.

In the subroutine, the first LOCATE statement sets the next printing position, and the first PRINT statement displays the arrow at that position. Then another FOR—NEXT loop counts from 1 to 100 in order to stall the program slightly. After the delay, the second LOCATE statement resets the printing position at the beginning of the arrow, and the second PRINT statement erases the arrow from the screen—except when x% equals 70. When x% equals 70, the arrow is not erased, so it stays on the screen after the program has ended.

Here is the output from Listing 9.1 (on your screen, however, the arrow moves):

```
    >>--->
```

Type in the first four lines of Listing 9.1, which make up the main program. When you're finished, your screen should look something like Fig. 1.

Fig.
1

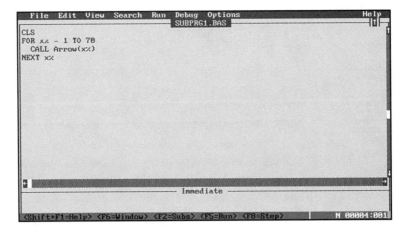

Now type the first line of the subroutine, which starts with the SUB keyword. When you press Enter at the end of the line, you'll get a surprise. Your screen instantly displays the window for the program's Arrow () subroutine, as shown in Fig. 2.

Fig.
2

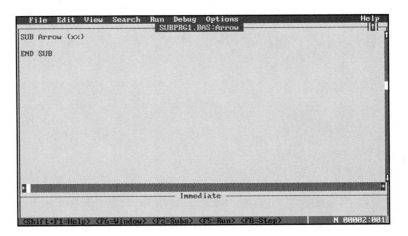

What happened? Did you press the wrong key on your keyboard? Did you forget to pay your electric bill? Because a subroutine is considered a separate module of your program, QBasic automatically gives it its own window. Moreover, because every subroutine must end with the END SUB statement, QBasic automatically adds that statement to your subroutine. All you have to do is type the subroutine's statements between the SUB and END SUB lines. Do that now, so your screen looks something like Fig. 3.

Fig. 3

```
  File  Edit  View  Search  Run  Debug  Options                    Help
                         SUBPRG1.BAS:Arrow
SUB Arrow (x%)
   LOCATE 5, x%
   PRINT ">>--->"
   FOR delay = 1 TO 100: NEXT delay
   LOCATE 5, x%
   IF x% < 70 THEN PRINT "        "
END SUB




                              Immediate
<Shift+F1=Help> <F6=Window> <F2=Subs> <F5=Run> <F8=Step>        N 00001:001
```

When you're finished typing, save the program as SUBPRG1.BAS, then press Shift-F5 to run the program and watch the little arrow zip across your screen.

You're probably wondering where the rest of your program went when the subroutine window appeared. You can easily get to any module of your program by selecting the SUBs... entry of the View menu, or by pressing F2. When you do, you see the SUBs dialog box, as shown in Fig. 4.

Fig.
4

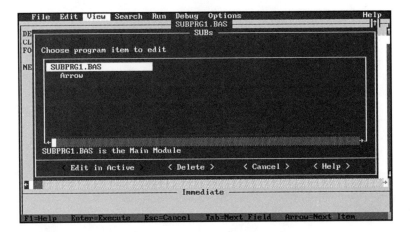

The program's main module is at the top of the module list, with other modules listed below. You can get to any module by double-clicking it with your mouse or by highlighting it with your arrow keys and pressing Enter. Notice also that this dialog box contains buttons for deleting modules from your program, should you ever need to do so.

Use the SUBs dialog box to get back to the main program. At the top of the program, you'll see the line DECLARE SUB Arrow (x%). Talk about the ghost in the machine! Where the heck did that line come from? Every program module, except the main module, must have a DECLARE line at the top of your program. Because QBasic is such a clever little puppy, it automatically adds the necessary DECLARE statements to your program when you save it. Thank-you letters may be addressed to Microsoft Corporation.

Now for the hundred-million dollar question: How does this program work? The program is divided into two modules. The first module is the main program, which includes the first four lines you typed. This module is called the main program because it is at the highest level of your top-down design. That is, no other module uses the main program, but the main program calls modules that are lower in level.

The second module in Listing 9.1 is the Arrow subroutine. This subroutine is run (called) by the main program, so the Arrow subroutine is considered to be one level down from the main program in the top-down design. The FOR–NEXT loop in the main program calls Arrow 70 times, once each time through the loop. When the main program calls Arrow, the code in Arrow executes. In other words, the program branches to the first line of Arrow and executes all the statements until it gets to the END SUB line. When it reaches the END SUB line, the program branches back to the main module, to the line after the subroutine call. Because the line following the subroutine call is the end of the FOR–NEXT loop, the program goes back to the top of the loop, increments x%, and calls Arrow yet again. This continues until the loop runs out, which is when x% becomes 71.

See the x% in the parentheses in the call to Arrow? This is a subroutine argument. Arguments in subroutines work just like the arguments you used when calling QBasic's built-in functions. You use arguments to pass into subroutines the values those subroutines need to do their jobs. For example, in Chapter 5 you learned to get a string's length by calling the LEN function like this: length% = LEN(s$). In this case, s$ is the function's argument, just as x% in the call to Arrow is Arrow's argument. You need to give Arrow this argument because Arrow has to know the current value of the loop-control variable. This value determines where the arrow is drawn, as you can see when you look at the code in the subroutine.

NOTE

A subroutine can have as many arguments as you like. But you must be sure that the arguments you specify in the subroutine's call exactly match the type and order of the arguments in the subroutine's SUB line. To use more than one argument in a subroutine, separate the arguments with commas. For example, to add the argument y! to the Arrow

continues

continued

call, you'd type CALL Arrow(x%, y!). Then, so that the arguments match, you must change the first line of Arrow to SUB Arrow (x%, y!). You can use different variable names in the SUB line, as long as they are the same type. In other words, using the arrow example, you can also type SUB Arrow(col%, length!). In the subroutine, you'd then use the variable names col% and length!, rather than the original x% and y!. Subroutines don't have to have arguments. To call a subroutine that has no arguments, you wouldn't need the parentheses. For example: CALL Arrow.

In the first line of code in the subroutine (not counting the SUB line), you'll see a strange, new command. The LOCATE statement moves the on-screen printing position to the row and column listed after the command. The row is the first value after the LOCATE keyword and is the number of characters down from the top to start printing. The second value (in this case x%) is the column, counting from the left, at which to start printing.

The first time the subroutine gets called, the LOCATE statement moves the printing position 5 characters down from the top and 1 character to the right (because x% equals 1). The next line, which is a PRINT statement, prints the arrow character string at the new screen position.

The do-nothing FOR–NEXT loop then keeps the computer counting from 1 to 100. This keeps the arrow on-screen for a while before the next LOCATE and PRINT statements erase it. (To make the arrow move faster, change the 100 in the FOR–NEXT loop to a smaller value, which shortens the delay. To make the arrow go slower, change the 100 to a larger value.) By calling the Arrow subroutine again and again, the arrow is repeatedly drawn and erased on the screen, each time one character closer to the right margin. This makes the arrow look as if it's moving.

That wasn't too tough, was it? Unfortunately, using subroutines is a little more complicated than it may appear from the preceding discussion. If you jump right in and try to write your own subroutines at this point, you'll run into trouble faster than a dog catches fleas in the springtime. Before you can write good subroutines, you must at least learn about something called *variable scope*. Coincidentally, variable scope is the next topic in this chapter.

Variable Scope

(Help for variables with bad breath)

Now that you know a little about subroutines, you should know how QBasic organizes variables between modules. You may wonder, for example, why x% must be an argument in the call to Arrow. Why couldn't you just use the variable x% in the subroutine? After all, they're part of the same program, right?

You need arguments in your subroutines because of something called variable scope, which determines whether program modules can "see" a specific variable. For example, if you were to change the program so that x% was not passed as an argument to Arrow, you'd get an Illegal function call error when the program tried to execute the first LOCATE statement in Arrow.

Here's why: A variable in one module is not accessible in another (unless it's shared, which you'll learn about in a minute). So, when you don't explicitly pass x% as an argument, the Arrow subroutine can't access it. Because the variable x% in the main program is no longer visible to the Arrow subroutine, the subroutine assumes that the x% in its LOCATE statement is a new variable. QBasic initializes all new numeric variables to 0, so the x% in Arrow is equal to 0. There is no such screen position as 5,0; the LOCATE statement generates an error.

In the preceding case, the `x%` in `Arrow` is local to `Arrow`. Just as the main program's `x%` cannot be seen in any module except the main program (it's local to the main program), `Arrow`'s `x%` cannot be seen in any module except `Arrow`. This may seem at first like a crazy way to do things, but when you think about it, it makes a lot of sense.

PLAY BALL!

BUZZWORD

Local and Global Variables

Local variables are those variables not accessible outside the module in which they appear. *Global variables*, on the other hand, are accessible anywhere within a program.

By not allowing a variable to be seen outside the module in which it's used, you never have to worry about some other module accidentally changing that variable's value. Moreover, local variables make subroutines self-contained modules, as if everything the subroutine needed were put together in a little box. If the value of a variable used in a subroutine is giving your program trouble, you know exactly which module to check. You don't need to search your entire program to find the problem any more than you need to search your entire house to find a quart of milk.

The opposite of a local variable is a global variable. Global variables can be used in any module anywhere in your program. Listing 9.2 is a new version of Listing 9.1, which makes `x%` a global variable. Because `x%` is now a global variable, it does not have to be passed as an argument.

Listing 9.2 SUBRTN2.BAS uses a global variable

Here **x%** is declared as —————— a shared (or global) variable

```
DECLARE SUB Arrow ()
DIM SHARED x%
CLS
FOR x% = 1 TO 70
```

Now the ──────────── CALL Arrow
subroutine   NEXT x%
has no
argument   SUB Arrow
                        LOCATE 5, x%
                        PRINT ">>--->"
                        FOR delay = 1 TO 100: NEXT delay
                        LOCATE 5, x%
                        IF x% < 70 THEN PRINT "   "
                      END SUB

IN SIMPLE TERMS

Listing 9.2 works almost exactly like Listing 9.1. The difference is that now x% is a global variable and does not have to be passed as an argument into Arrow().

The DIM SHARED line (the first line) in Listing 9.2 is the statement that allows x% to be used inside the Arrow subroutine without having to pass it as an argument. By declaring x% this way, it becomes a global variable, one that can be accessed by any module in your program.

TIP

As a novice programmer, you may think that using global variables is a great programming shortcut. After all, if you make all your variables global, you'll never have to worry about passing arguments to subroutines. However, a program with lots of global variables is a poorly designed program—hard to read and hard to debug. You should write your programs to include as few global variables as possible.

QBASIC FOR ROOKIES

Using Functions

(Still more blocks in the pyramid)

You can also break your programs into modules using functions. But unlike subroutines, functions always return a value to the main program. You've used QBasic functions before in this book, such as the LEN() function. The value it returns is the number of characters in a string.

You write functions much like subroutines. However, function calls must assign the function's return value to a variable. Suppose you have a function named GetNum% that gets a number from the user and returns it to your program. A call to the function might look something like this: num% = GetNum%. (Notice that the function name includes a symbol that tells you the function's return type. Any function name that doesn't include a type symbol returns a single-precision number.) Listing 9.3 is a short program that illustrates how to use functions in your QBasic programs.

Listing 9.3 FUNCTION.BAS includes a function module

```
                    DECLARE FUNCTION GetInput$ ()
                    CLS
Function call ──────  response$ = GetInput$
                    LOCATE 2, 1
                    PRINT "You typed '"; response$; ".'"

                    FUNCTION GetInput$
                      LOCATE 20, 1
                      PRINT "  PLEASE ENTER TEXT BELOW"
                      PRINT "--------------------------------"
                      PRINT " > "
                      PRINT "--------------------------------"
                      LOCATE 22, 3
                      LINE INPUT s$
                      GetInput$ = s$
                    END FUNCTION
```

IN SIMPLE TERMS

The main program in Listing 9.3 first clears the screen, then calls the function `GetInput$` to get a string from the user. This string is stored in the string variable `s$`. After getting the string, the main program uses `LOCATE` to set the next screen printing position, and then displays the string the user typed.

The function `GetInput$` sets the screen's printing position and prints an input box in which the user can enter his string. The `LINE INPUT` statement retrieves the string from the user, after which the string is returned by the function.

When you run Listing 9.3, the program prints a fancy input box on the screen (well, fancy to folks who prefer Big Macs to filet mignon) and asks you to enter a string. When you enter the string, the program shows you what you typed, just in case you forget what it was—or maybe just to verify that the function did indeed return the string to the main program. Fig. 5 shows the output of Listing 9.3.

Fig. 5

```
You typed 'This is a test.'



















   PLEASE ENTER TEXT BELOW
------------------------------------------
 >This is a test
------------------------------------------

Press any key to continue
```

Refer back to the main program first. At the top, a DECLARE statement declares the GetInput$ function. You don't actually have to type this line. QBasic inserts the line automatically when you save the program. A little further down in the main program, you can see the line response$ = GetInput$, which is the call to the GetInput$ function. When the program gets to this point, it branches to the first line of the GetInput$ function. The GetInput$ function prints the input box on the screen and retrieves the input from the user.

The only thing in GetInput$ that you haven't seen before is the LINE INPUT command, which is a handy way to get strings. LINE INPUT works much like a regular INPUT statement, except you use it only to get strings, and it doesn't print a question mark on the screen.

Just before the END FUNCTION line (which is how you always end a function module) is the line GetInput$ = s$. This assignment statement is where the string retrieved from the user is returned from the function to the main program. On the left of the assignment operator is the function's name, and on the right is the value to return from the function. All functions return their values this way. If, for example, you had a function called GetValue% that returned an integer, somewhere in your GetValue% function must be a line like GetValue% = value%, where value% is the value being returned from the function.

As you can see, functions are similar to subroutines. In fact, you can pass arguments to functions the same way you do to subroutines. Just add parentheses to the function's name and list the arguments, separated by commas, inside the parentheses. Don't forget to match the arguments in the function's call with those in the function's FUNCTION line. For example, the function call s$ = GetStr$(prompt$) must call a function whose first line is FUNCTION GetStr$ (prompt$). (Actually, the variable prompt$ in the FUNCTION line can have any name, as long as it's the same variable type as the argument in the function call.)

Now, you've come to the part of the book that separates the men from the boys, the women from the girls, and the butterflies from the caterpillars. Are you ready? Because it's time to take a look at...

... The Final Program

(One last spin around the block)

Listing 9.4, the last program in this book, is an example of a modular program. It also summarizes much of what you've learned in this book. (If that doesn't impress you, maybe the fact that it's a game will get you to type it.) Because Listing 9.4 is much larger than other programs you've seen, it's a pretty big typing task. Be careful to type everything correctly. Otherwise, the program may not run properly.

Listing 9.4 GALLERY.BAS is a shooting gallery game

```
DECLARE SUB ShowScore (score%)
DECLARE FUNCTION PlayGame% ()
DECLARE SUB EraseTarget (target.position%)
DECLARE SUB ShootArrow (a%, target.position%)
DECLARE FUNCTION ShowTarget% ()
DECLARE SUB DrawScreen ()

RANDOMIZE TIMER        'Seed random number generator.
CALL DrawScreen        'Draw the playing screen.
score% = PlayGame%     'Play the game.
CALL ShowScore(score%) 'Show the final score.

SUB DrawScreen
  CLS
  FOR x% = 1 TO 10
    LOCATE x% * 2 + 2, 1
    PRINT "-------------------------------------------------------"
```

FOR-NEXT loop prints one lane wall and one arrow each time through the loop

continues

Listing 9.4 Continued

```
        IF x% < 10 THEN
          LOCATE x% * 2 + 3, 1
          PRINT x%; ">>-->"
        END IF
      NEXT x%
    END SUB

    SUB EraseTarget (target.position%)
      LOCATE target.position% * 2 + 3, 60
      PRINT " "
    END SUB

    FUNCTION PlayGame%
      score% = 0
      FOR x% = 1 TO 25
        target.position% = ShowTarget%
        start.time& = TIMER
        shot.fired% = 0

        DO
          a% = VAL(INKEY$)
          IF a% >= 1 AND a% <= 9 THEN
            CALL ShootArrow(a%, target.position%)
            shot.fired% = 1
          END IF
        LOOP UNTIL (shot.fired%) OR (TIMER > start.time& + 1)

        IF a% = target.position% THEN
          BEEP
          score% = score% + 1
        END IF

        CALL EraseTarget(target.position%)
      NEXT x%
      PlayGame% = score%
    END FUNCTION
```

This loop gives you 25 targets

Starting time is saved here

Keep trying to get keystrokes until the player shoots or one second goes by

This part of the code is executed when the player hits the target

The score is returned from the function here

Each time
through the
loop, the
arrow moves
one character
to the right

```
SUB ShootArrow (a%, target.position%)
  FOR x% = 4 TO 60
    LOCATE a% * 2 + 3, x%
    PRINT ">>-->"
    FOR delay = 1 TO 50: NEXT delay
    LOCATE a% * 2 + 3, x%
    PRINT "        "
  NEXT x%
  LOCATE a% * 2 + 3, 4
  PRINT ">>-->"
END SUB

SUB ShowScore (score%)
  LOCATE 20, 60
  PRINT "--------------------"
  LOCATE 21, 60
  PRINT "  Your score is"; score%
  LOCATE 22, 60
  PRINT "--------------------"
END SUB
```

This random
number is the
lane in which
the target will
appear

```
FUNCTION ShowTarget%
  p% = INT(9 * RND + 1)
  LOCATE p% * 2 + 3, 60
  PRINT "X"
  ShowTarget% = p%
END FUNCTION
```

When you run Listing 9.4, it draws a simple shooting gallery on your
screen, as shown in Fig. 6.

The gallery is made up of nine lanes, each containing an arrow. When
the program starts, a target (an X) appears to the right of the lanes. Your
task is to shoot the target with one of your arrows. To fire an arrow, press
the lane's number. You have to be fast because the target moves quickly.
After 25 targets have appeared, the game ends, and your final score is

displayed. If the score is not as high as you'd like, you can either throw a tantrum or try again.

Fig.
6

```
---------------------------------------------------------
 1 >>--->          --------------------------------------
 2 >>--->          --------------------------------------
 3                         >>--->                   X
                   --------------------------------------
 4 >>--->          --------------------------------------
 5 >>--->          --------------------------------------
 6 >>--->          --------------------------------------
 7 >>--->          --------------------------------------
 8 >>--->          --------------------------------------
 9 >>--->          --------------------------------------
```

Because of the size of Listing 9.4, there's no "In Simple Terms" box describing how it works. In a way, this program is your final exam. Go through it line by line, figuring out how it does what it does. Analyzing programs is a skill you should develop if you plan to continue programming.

Before you get started, there are a few things in Listing 9.4 you haven't seen before. First, near the top of the program is the line RANDOMIZE TIMER. This line initializes QBasic's random-number generator. The program uses random numbers to select the target's next position on the screen. Failure to initialize the random-number generator results in the same series of "random" numbers every time you run the program, which makes for a boring game. To initialize, or *seed*, the random-number generator, you must give RANDOMIZE a different value each time you run the program. Because TIMER represents the number of seconds since midnight, and therefore is different each time you run the program, it's perfect for this task.

BUZZWORD

Seed

Most random-number generators use a seed value to get started. If you use the same seed value to initialize the generator, you'll always get the same series of numbers. Random numbers in a computer are not truly random, but rather are calculated by a formula. Luckily, by using a different seed value every time you run a program, you can simulate true random numbers, since you can't predict the series of numbers that will be created by the formula.

In the main program, notice that some lines end with an apostrophe followed by a line of text. These are comments. Comments are little notes to yourself (or whoever ends up reading your program) to explain what the program does. You can use comments to document your program. When QBasic sees the apostrophe, it knows that the rest of the line is a comment and ignores it. If you like, you can have an entire block of lines that are nothing but comments. QBasic won't even care if you put a letter to Uncle Henry in the middle of your program, as long as each line starts with an apostrophe.

The rest of the main program contains nothing new. However, in the function PlayGame%, you'll see the line a% = VAL(INKEY$). You already know that VAL returns the numeric value of a number string, but what the heck is that INKEY$? INKEY$ checks the keyboard for a keypress. If the user has pressed a key, INKEY$ returns the key's character to your program. If the user hasn't yet pressed a key, INKEY$ returns a null (empty) string.

This program uses INKEY$ to read keystrokes "on the fly," without forcing the program to stop for input as it does with a regular INPUT statement. By enclosing the call to INKEY$ within a DO loop, the program constantly polls the keyboard (checks the keyboard for input) at the same time it

checks to see if your time for the current target has run out. The DO loop ends if the user presses a key or if a second has passed since the loop started.

In the function ShowTarget%, you can see where the random numbers are generated. The line p% = INT(9 * RND +1) generates a random number from 1 to 9. The program uses this random number to determine where to print the next target on the screen. Look at this line of code carefully, because it's a little tricky.

First, the QBasic function RND returns a random number between 0 and 1. In order to get this random number in the range you need for the program, you must apply the formula INT(N * RND + 1), which returns a value from 1 to N. In Listing 9.4, you want a value from 1 to 9, so N equals 9. If you wanted random numbers from 1 to 100, you'd write p% = INT(100 * RND + 1). (Of course, p% is just a variable name; you could use any variable name you wanted.) The function INT converts the value inside the parentheses to an integer, so you don't end up with a number like 5.347324.

Everything else in Listing 9.4 should be familiar to you. If you have trouble figuring out a section of the code, try to think like a computer, taking the program one line at a time and making sure you know what each line does. If you do, you'll have no trouble figuring out the entire program.

Program Debugging

(Get the Raid!)

As your programs get longer, you'll discover that finding errors can be difficult and confusing. Often, something will go wrong with your program, and you'll have no idea where to look for the problem. This can

lead to sleepless nights, a bad disposition, and the inability to eat pizza for breakfast. Luckily, QBasic includes a simple debugger that can help you find programming errors. The commands that control the debugger are found in the Debug menu shown in Fig. 7.

Fig. 7

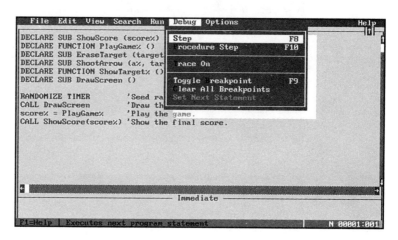

The first command in the Debug menu is **Step**, which allows you to step through your program one line at a time. Each time you select this command (the easiest way is to press F8), your program executes a single line of code and then stops.

To see how this works, load Listing 9.4 into QBasic, and then press F8. The program highlights the line RANDOMIZE TIMER and stops, as shown in Fig. 8.

The highlighted line is the next line the computer will execute. Press F8; the RANDOMIZE line is executed, and the next line in your program is highlighted. Because this line is a call to the subroutine DrawScreen, the program branches to the first line of the subroutine when you press F8 again. Press F8 now, and your screen will look something like Fig. 9. As you can see, when a subroutine or function call is executed, the **Step** command highlights the first line of the new module.

Fig.
8

```
  File  Edit  View  Search  Run  Debug  Options                    Help
                          GALLERY.BAS
 DECLARE SUB ShowScore (score%)
 DECLARE FUNCTION PlayGame% ()
 DECLARE SUB EraseTarget (target.position%)
 DECLARE SUB ShootArrow (a%, target.position%)
 DECLARE FUNCTION ShowTarget% ()
 DECLARE SUB DrawScreen ()

 RANDOMIZE TIMER          'Seed random number generator.
 CALL DrawScreen          'Draw the playing screen.
 score% = PlayGame%       'Play the game.
 CALL ShowScore(score%)   'Show the final score.




                         ─ Immediate ─
 <Shift+F1=Help> <F5=Continue> <F9=Toggle Bkpt> <F8=Step>    N 00008:001
```

Fig.
9

```
  File  Edit  View  Search  Run  Debug  Options                    Help
                     GALLERY.BAS:DrawScreen
 SUB DrawScreen
   CLS
   FOR x% = 1 TO 10
     LOCATE x% * 2 + 2, 1
     PRINT "_____"
     IF x% < 10 THEN
       LOCATE x% * 2 + 3, 1
       PRINT x%; ">>-->"
     END IF
   NEXT x%
 END SUB




                         ─ Immediate ─
 <Shift+F1=Help> <F5=Continue> <F9=Toggle Bkpt> <F8=Step>    N 00002:003
```

Press F8 until the line NEXT x% is highlighted. At this point, the program
has drawn only a small part of the game's screen. But where is the
screen? To see what the program has drawn so far, press F4 to switch to
the output screen. Your screen should look something like Fig. 10.

Fig.
10

```
--------------------------------------------------------
1 >>—>
```

When you're stepping through a program, you can do more than just examine the output screen. You can also check the values of variables. (You can even check your socks for holes, but this is unlikely to help with your programming.) For example, suppose you want to know the value of x% at this point in your program. First, press F6 to activate the Immediate window. Then type PRINT x% and press Enter. The output screen appears, with the current value of x% displayed right below the other program output. Because the program has gone through the loop only once, this value is 1, just as it should be.

To get a little practice with the Step command, keep pressing F8 to step through the loop. Periodically, press F4 to switch to the output screen and see what's been printed so far. Also, use the Immediate window to check the value of the loop-control variable x%, which should increase until it reaches 11.

The next command in the **D**ebug menu, **P**rocedure Step, allows you to run a subroutine or function without stepping through each line of the function. For example, in Listing 9.4 if you select the **P**rocedure Step command (F10) when the line CALL DrawScreen is highlighted, QBasic

executes the DrawScreen subroutine, drawing the entire playing screen without stopping. After drawing the screen, the program stops on the line score% = PlayGame%.

The Trace On command in the Debug menu lets you run your program in slow motion. To use this option, first select Trace On in the Debug menu. A small dot appears next to the Trace On menu item. Now press Shift-F5 to run your program from the start. QBasic starts executing your program one line at a time, much as it did when you used the Step command, except now you don't need to keep pressing F8. To stop the trace, press Ctrl-Break. You can then check the value of any variables or examine your program's output up to that point.

Sometimes you may want your program to run up to a certain point and then stop. For example, suppose you want to check the value of a% after the line a% = VAL(INKEY$) in the function PlayGame% executes. To do this, first bring the PlayGame% function up on your screen. Then move the window's text cursor to the line immediately following the line you want to check. (In this case, you want to place the cursor on the IF statement following the line a% = VAL(INKEY$).) Now, select the Toggle Breakpoint command in the Debug menu, or just press F9. The line you selected turns red (shown shaded in Fig. 11) and is now selected as a breakpoint. Setting breakpoints is a fast way to stop your program on a specific line.

Press Shift-F5 to run the program. Almost immediately, the program stops on the breakpoint line. You can now inspect the variable a%, which should be 0 since you haven't had a chance to press a key yet.

You can set as many breakpoints as you like in your program. To clear a breakpoint, place the text cursor on the breakpoint line and press F9 again to toggle the red highlight off. To clear all breakpoints in a program simultaneously, select Clear All Breakpoints from the Debug menu.

Fig. 11

```
 File  Edit  View  Search  Run  Debug  Options                    Help
                     GALLERY.BAS:PlayGame
FUNCTION PlayGame%
   score% = 0
   FOR x% = 1 TO 25
      target.position% = ShowTarget%
      start.time& = TIMER
      shot.fired% = 0

      DO
        a% = VAL(INKEY$)
        IF a% >= 1 AND a% <= 9 THEN
          CALL ShootArrow(a%, target.position%)
          shot.fired% = 1
        END IF
      LOOP UNTIL (shot.fired%) OR (TIMER > start.time& + 1)

      IF a% = target.position% THEN
        BEEP
        score% = score% + 1

                       Immediate
<Shift+F1=Help>  <F5=Continue>  <F9=Toggle Bkpt>  <F8=Step>       N 00010:007
```

The last command in the **D**ebug menu is Set **N**ext Statement. This command allows you to choose any line in your program as the next line to execute. This can be handy when you want to skip over a block of code. To set the next statement to execute, place the text cursor on the line you want to execute, and then select the Set **N**ext Statement command in the **D**ebug menu. QBasic highlights the selected line. When the program begins again, the selected line is the next to execute.

Using QBasic's debugger to trace your program's flow and to check the value of variables makes finding programming errors a lot less frustrating. Because you're not likely to ever write a perfect program, developing good debugging skills is as important as learning to program in the first place.

Common Rookie Mistakes

Writing lengthy modules. Programs are broken into small modules in order to make program code easier to understand. To this end, each module in

a program should perform only a single task, so it stays short and to the point. When you try to cram too much functionality into a module, it loses its identity. If you can't state a module's purpose in two or three words, it's probably doing too much.

Confusing local and global variables. Remember that if you haven't declared a variable as shared, it is accessible only in the module in which it appears. This means that you can have two or more variables with the same name in a program, all holding different values. Use arguments to pass variables between modules. Use global variables only when unavoidable.

Confusing subroutines and functions. If you need to return a value from a module, use a function. If you're not returning a value, use a subroutine.

Mixing up the order of arguments. You can pass one or more arguments to subroutines and functions. However, keep in mind that the arguments are passed to the module in the order in which they appear in the module call. The module's SUB or FUNCTION line should list the arguments in the same order they are listed in the module call.

Summing Up

▼ Modular programming means breaking a program into a series of simple tasks.

▼ Top-down programming means organizing modules in a hierarchy, with general-purpose modules at the top that call specific-purpose modules lower in the hierarchy. A program written this way can be thought of as a pyramid, with the main program at the top. The further down the pyramid you go, the more specific in function the modules become.

▼ Subroutines and functions are the two types of modules you can use when writing a QBasic program. Functions must return values, while subroutines do not.

▼ The LOCATE statement allows you to set the screen position for the next PRINT statement.

▼ Local variables are accessible only within the module in which they appear. Global variables are accessible anywhere in a program. The DIM SHARED statement declares a global variable.

▼ The LINE INPUT statement works much like INPUT, except that it can be used only to input strings and it does not display a question mark.

▼ To get random numbers, you must first use the RANDOMIZE statement to seed the random-number generator. The RND function then returns a random number between 0 and 1.

▼ The INKEY$ function checks for a keypress and returns the key's character if a key was pressed or a null string if no key was pressed.

▼ QBasic's debugger steps through your program in various ways, allowing you to watch the order in which statements are executed and to check the values of variables at different points in your program.

Always More to Learn

(Groan)

You've now reached the end of *QBasic for Rookies*. (Stop cheering, please.) If you've read each lesson carefully, you should have a good idea

of what computer programming is all about. But there's much more you need to know if you want to pursue programming as a profession or even as a serious hobby. Don't stop your studies with this book. Two books you might want to check out are *QBasic By Example* by Greg Perry and *Using BASIC* by Phil Feldman and Tom Rugg, both published by Que. Either of these fine texts will provide excellent training in more advanced BASIC programming.

Regardless of where your studies lead you, there is nothing more important when learning a new skill than practice. Reading a book is only the first step. To really understand the art of programming, you must program—a lot. The more programs you design and write, the better programmer you'll become. Don't be afraid to experiment with your programs. There's nothing you can do with QBasic that will damage your computer. If you're willing to put in the time and effort, you'll soon amaze yourself and your friends with the wonderful things you can make your computer do.

Index

Symbols

A

B